by Joe Pace

Moss

Reliquary Press
13920 Sunfish Bend Alpharetta GA 30004

www.reliquarypress.com

ISBN: 978-1-936519-99-6
Printed in the United States of America
Reliquary Press rev. date: 12/6/2021
Cover design by Bill Coffin

Dedication

*For fathers and sons
I have the best of both*

Acknowledgements

Every book is a collaborative effort, and I am deeply grateful for all of those who helped take Moss from an idea to the printed page.

For my readers, who made the novel better with their critiques and their suggestions: Seth O'Donnell, Mary Walsh, Karen Kilrain Bast, Amanda Horvath, Greg Brown, Tim MacKinnon, Diana Pankowski, Laurie Watts, Amy Farnham, Roger Goun, Kathy Slade, Mary Clancy, Carla and Steve Billingham, Anthony Zizos, and Maia LaVallee. And for Lionel Ingram, who nudged the facts of my military history into place.

For my friends from the publishing world who shared their advice and sympathy: Jacquelyn Benson, Emily Baker, and Chris Swann.

For Derrick Eisenhardt, who believed in this book.

For my writing partner Bill Coffin, who has been there every step of the way, and who understands these characters in his marrow. Thanks, Bill. For everything.

And for my wife Sarah, who listened to every word and helped me find the truth in them.

CHAPTER ONE

I wasn't surprised when my father died. Old men die. And whatever else he was, my father was old. Eighty-seven, I think, and probably older than that inside from a lifetime spent in the indulgence of his three great loves. The first was white-label Jim Beam, and they were inseparable after my father found his taste for bourbon in Korea during the War. He referred to Korea as the Shit-sock of Asia, with that talent for indelible phrases which had made him such a celebrated success at his second passion, the written word. Yeah, my father was Isaiah Moss, *that* Isaiah Moss, the one who wrote those novels the critics loved, even the strutting bleeding-agate types who never liked anything if three other people liked it too. He was that rare author who straddled the great chasm between commercial success and critical acclaim; most lists for the best novels of the 20th century include two of his books. Sometimes three. What that really means is that he became a literary legend and a cultural icon, all while making a fortune.

I hated my father.

His third great love, after drinking and writing, was women. He couldn't get enough, and there was a steady parade of them throughout his celebrated fucking career. As you would expect, a man with his celebrity and wealth never lacked for attractive young company. There was always some new young thing ready to hike up her skirt for Isaiah Moss, either for the notoriety or in the hope that she might become the future former Mrs. Moss, with all the financial security that would imply. Vain hope, that. My father never married, not even my mother. Especially not my mother. The virtual entirety of his adult life was spent with his hands on a typewriter or between firm thighs, and my father was fond of boasting that never did the same thing twice. Not in the bedroom, and certainly not on the page. I wish I could sit here and tell you that I knew in my heart that my mother was his favorite, the true love of his life, but that would be bullshit, and one of the many pieces of advice the old man dispensed to his only son was that lies made for bad writing. So here I am, telling you the truth about a man I never loved, never even really knew, and getting it out of the way early, so you know this isn't some fairy tale. Because it's not.

My mother was twenty when I was born, and my father was forty-five. He sent us checks, sufficiently fat that there was enough food on the table and new shoes for me every year, and she could abandon her fiction of a career as an actress. As big of a self-absorbed asshole as he was, Isaiah Moss seemed tickled that he had a child. We met only once, and as I was just a few days old my memories of the visit are understandably scanty. The sum total of his fatherly attention came in the form of money and, perhaps not surprisingly, letters. They would arrive with some frequency throughout my childhood, perhaps once a month, tapering to two or maybe three a year once I went to college. They were odd, rambling missives, full of a kind of broken stream of consciousness from one of the foremost American novelists of his generation. There was some vague paternal advice, occasional tips on how to attract beautiful women (these generally included some variation on "be a famous writer"), and a lot of fragmentary dialogue that suggested he and James Beam had been spending time together. Some were a paragraph or two, some were virtual novellas. The worst part was that the passages were almost always brilliant. Even tapping out drunken throwaway pages to his seldom-seen offspring, the man was a towering talent.

Like I said, I hated him.

The bitch of it is that I was a writer too. Not at my father's level, but that's not a level, that's a pantheon of gods sitting atop Olympus peppering the mortals below with literary thunderbolts. I'd been writing since I could remember. In elementary school we had those little competitions where you would "publish" your best work by stitching it between two pieces of cardboard and covering it with wallpaper. I won three years in a row – it was in the local paper with a picture and everything. I don't know what happened the fourth year. Then it was scribbling in notebooks and a series of high school English teachers with no idea about my celebrated lineage waxing poetical about my potential in comments home to my mom. She neither encouraged or discouraged me, but instead would hug me in her pillowy grasp and tell me she would love me if I became a cab driver. That was her phrase, "Oscar Kendall, I will love you even if you become a cab driver." Kendall was her last name, and she gave it to me. The Oscar came from my father, who thought he was the more talented and more heterosexual reincarnation of Oscar Wilde. Of course, that gave me the soporific initials O.K., which might sound cool, but who wants to be just O.K.? I wanted to be more than O.K., even though I suspected deep down that it was probably all I could aspire to.

I'm not sure just what she had against cab drivers, my mom, but her unconditional love remained one of the simple and enduring foundations of my life. She was never an intellectual giant, which is part of how I know she could never have been the love of my father's life. I've seen pictures, seen how gorgeous she was as a young model. Long black cascades of hair, feline eyes, an hourglass figure that would never run out of sand. I remember when I first became aware that my mother was sexy. I was nine and we were at the beach, sitting on a sprawling towel and eating ice cream. My mother was wearing a two-piece, not even a particularly provocative one, navy blue with white polka dots. Eating ice cream with her kid. And yet strange men made it a point to let their gaze linger, and a few even stopped by to say hello, emboldened by the lack of a wedding ring on my mother's finger. My mom was polite to them all, but it never moved beyond politeness. It was a breezy day, not cold but not hot, and I noticed the hardness of my mother's nipples through the fabric of her top. Something in my juvenile awareness made the connection between the overtime her suit was putting in and the masculine traffic at our blanket. None of them, to my recollection, stopped to ask what books she liked to read. I know what Isaiah Moss wanted from Peggy

Kendall nine months before I was born, and it wasn't literary repartee.

I kept writing, kept filling those notebooks, throughout high school and college and even now, even as forty came and went and the furtive secret scribbling that had once been precocious became pathetic. My mother gave me dark hair and decent bone structure, and my father gave me a bottomless well of words. Words usually came easily from that well, flowing fluidly from my mind to my hands to the page, though where he had been a typewriter man, I preferred lined paper and pens. Blue pens, always, never black. Boxes and bins of those notebooks lurk in the basement at my mother's little house in Connecticut, full of words no one has ever seen and probably never will. Unfinished novels, half-glimpsed scenes, nebulous characters. I don't need some armchair psychologist to tell me why I never finish anything, why I've never sought an agent or publisher, let alone my father's baleful author's eye while he was alive. I know why. Good as it is (and with the inherent conceit of the writer, I like to tell myself it is good), it's not as good as his stuff. Whose is? This is Isaiah Moss we're talking about, heir to Hemingway and Steinbeck, peer of Vonnegut and Updike, an immortal. Stupid, sure, but there was this part of me that dreamed of the day I'd write the perfect book. I'd send it to him, not for his love or approval, but so he would know that his son was better than he was, that Hercules had outstripped Zeus. The rest of me, the rational majority, knew this was ridiculous. And so the three straight wallpaper-wrapped classics remain the entirety of my published works.

I don't know why I kept doing it. I didn't enjoy it. It was agony, and it shouldn't be. Writing should be a joyful exercise, even when it's work. The ejaculation of words onto the page should include some pleasure, or at least a cathartic measure of release, but for me it has always been just the agony. Suffused with the knowledge of my permanent inferiority, I trudged on nevertheless, sending sentences into an ether I knew would never respond, never judge, never dismiss. I kept writing not out of love but out of inability not to, and the notebooks piled up, missives to the darkness, dreams unrealized, godhood deferred. And I could keep telling myself that it was good.

Because nobody pays advances or royalties on wallpaper-covered books written by eight-year-olds, in waking life I made my living as a high school literature teacher at Arcadia, an elite-and-well-aware-of-it private school. Nestled in the maple-lined avenues of southern Maryland just a silver-dollar's toss from the District of Columbia, Arcadia was a repository for the precious progeny of senators and the lobbyists who loved them. Diplomats and cabinet secretaries and professional sports team owners and the titans of corporate America sent us their well-dressed scions of privilege and we sanded down their rough academic edges a bit so they could ride the escalator to Georgetown and Harvard and Stanford, and then on up to whatever genteel legacied success awaited. Teaching was as comfortable a place as any to hide while I told myself I was a writer, and teaching paid the bills. Isaiah Moss's largesse had included footing the bill for my four undergrad years at Dartmouth, but he harbored the quaintly old-fashioned opinion that a man should make his own way in the world. One of his letters to me, in March of my senior year at Hanover, told me what I could expect of him after graduation:

Your classmates' fathers will undoubtedly be expressing their pride to their spawn in the weeks and months ahead. Dullard plumbers, proud of their engineers, as though it were their accomplishment, as though some detached vital organ of theirs trod the commencement stage. I have never been proud of you. Not once. Why should I be proud? Your achievements, now and in the days to come, grand or feeble as they may be, are yours, not mine. I never swung your bat or kissed one of your little girlfriends or opened your chemistry textbook. I wrote checks, I purchased your health and your tuition. These were not investments made looking forward, with any anticipation of future dividends. I do not desire or rely upon some future familial bond or support in my dotage (when I require a nursemaid, mine will be far, far more attractive than you). These payments have instead been the extirpation of debts incurred via a handful of pleasurable nights in the company of your mother some months before your squalling debut. A child is blameless in the nature of the assignation of its parents, and so I took it upon myself to pay for my crimes. You are a grown man now, or at least at the threshold of such, and my onus is at an end. I am paroled.

Men will also be bragging to their sons about their love for them. To this, perhaps, they can lay greater claim than the absurdity of pride. I do not love you. I do not know you, beyond a passing superficiality. I think your mother loves you. Content yourself with that.

Love, anyway, bores me.

Enclosed is some money. Spend it on a girl.

~~~

I was at Arcadia when I found out about his death, at work but not really working. Out on the front steps of Casper Hall between classes, I sat on cool a cool granite stair unwarmed by the unenthusiasm of an uncharacteristically pale late-spring Maryland sun. It was my favorite spot on campus, the perfect place to smoke when they still allowed it. I didn't quit because they said my spot was too close to the building and took it away, along with all the other spots like it on campus, but it had made the quitting easier. Most of my cigarettes each day had been there on those steps. I still sat there at times throughout the day, following the schedule if not the full habits of the longtime nicotine addict. To my mind the massive granite steps had long ago molded to the curve of my ass, and it remained a perfect place, if not to smoke then to sit, to watch the periodic streams of prosperous young men and women bustle through the courtyard. When the clockwork crowds ceased, and the scenery subsided once again to trees and grass and paving stones, I would return to the student papers I was grading or writing samples I was reading. When I grew tired of their tortured syntax, I would turn to one of the yellow legal pads I always had with me to conduct some torture of my own. Yellow legal pads, never white, and always a felt-tipped blue pen. A pen should scratch against the paper, there should be friction. A man should know when he's writing; it should be a physical act with resistance against the fingers. Ball point pens were too smooth, too easy, and laptop computers were too pregnant with convenient distractions. I stared at the pad, feeling the familiar scant weight of it in my hands. Sometimes there would be writing there, scrawled words in vivid blue decipherable only to me. My handwriting was execrable. If we were living in a Henny Youngman joke from the 1950's, my mother would complain about her son's terrible handwriting without even the excuse of being a doctor. Sometimes the words were inspired prose, sometimes classroom reminders or shopping lists, and sometimes there was nothing on the page but inane doodles. Not infrequently, as now, the pad was blank.

I set it aside and returned to the pile of creative writing papers by my juniors and thumbed through it, glancing at the names at their tops. With most of them, I knew what I was in for. Ceclia Gill's impeccable cursive would gush about a girl with boy problems, and Kelsie Brower would give me scantily researched historical fiction about heroic women. Nicholas Kentner would tell me a blood-drenched story about murder wasps or murder cowboys or murder hobos. I didn't mind Nick's stuff so much. He could make me laugh. I'd find something encouraging to say to all of them, even if I'd be begging for murder hobos to put me out of my misery before I finished.

The last paper in the pile was from Anh Meyer.

Anh Meyer.

I held it for a minute, just staring at it. Hers was always typed, which I'd long ago demanded because her handwriting was the abysmal scratching of poultry seeking something in the dirt. I'd never met a more confident, more exhausting student in my years of teaching. Very short and very thin, her legs no more than plastic straws sticking out from her blue Arcadia uniform skirt, Anh had been born in her native Vietnam and promptly deposited in an orphanage. Before turning two she was adopted by the Meyers, a childless and prominent Jewish couple both of whom were big wheels helping the D.C. public relations mill churn. Anh was no public relations slouch herself. All year she'd told me (and anyone else in earshot) how good a writer she was, and how she planned to be a great international novelist before she was thirty.

Her parents were professional shills, probably the type to tell her that self-promotion is the key to life. She must have listened, because she stood up in my hot classroom the first day that previous September and announced, tiny chin jutting out like the beak of a hummingbird, that before I retired I'd be assigning her books for students to read. I wanted to laugh and puke at the same time.

Girl, don't fool yourself, I thought. Then I read her first submission.

Anh Meyer could write.

She wrote with a singular, authentic voice that was unlike anything else I'd read before. It was still juvenile in places, heck, she was sixteen, but there were sustained stretches of prose that brought me to tears against my will. I wanted to hate every word, to be able to sit her down and gently let her know just how much work there was ahead of her to become even a competent writer, let alone a professional one. And that she could probably forget about dreams of world fame. Instead, I was left with the daunting realization that at sixteen, she was probably a better natural writer than I would ever be.

God, I hated her for that. Almost as much as I hated my father.

I knew how to drag a struggling student up to scratch, how to pick out what they did well and give them plenty of time to find their way to basic mediocrity. And I knew how to take a middling student and show them some rungs they could climb. I even knew how to take a talented kid and work with them on the next steps in a craft in which they showed promise. Hey, that's teaching, right? That's the gig, and sometimes I even enjoyed it. What I didn't know how to do was sit a Derby winner. Anh Meyer was going to be a novelist. She'd said as much, and she had the chops to back it up. That, I had no idea what to do with.

I sat there on my bench in the courtyard and read the last thing she'd write for me that year, her final draft of a story she'd authored dramatizing her own life's story. It was her best work yet. What little guidance I'd been able to provide she'd immediately incorporated, and in some cases she ignored my suggestions and her story was better for that, too. She took me through the death of each of her four grandparents in the war, through her mother's life in the sex trade, to her abandonment in Hanoi. It was scintillating. I was suffused by envy, ugly and shameful, envy of my student, envy of this girl who had gone from the orphanage to this kind of expressive brilliance in less time than it took me to fill a legal pad with garbage. My hand shook a little as I held her pages. I wished I still smoked so I could light it on fire.

I stood with a sigh, turning toward the ashtray that was no longer there to dispose of the cigarette that was not in my hand. No one had stopped to talk to me during my time on the steps that morning, which was unusual. Three or four times a day I would assume my perch in front of Casper Hall, almost always joined at some point by a colleague or a student. In the old days, I would share a smoke with them. The faculty, not the students. At least, usually not.

For ten years I had been sitting on those steps. I was still in my early forties, but I had achieved the distinction of becoming an institution without getting old. I kind of liked that. I enjoyed dispensing advice in the courtyard like some mountaintop Eastern guru; I even liked when students came to complain about exams or grades or some other grievance. Our previous Head of School at Arcadia, an elbow-patch academic throwback improbably named Cabot Rutledge had once groused that Oscar Kendall could be mistaken for a gargoyle on those steps, and if he wanted statuary in front of Casper Hall, he would commission it himself, and he would select something far more impressive. I outlasted that Head.

I had outlasted three. With one singular exception, Heads of School were ephemera.

A few days remained in the spring term at Arcadia School, the closing days of my tenth year teaching and rotting in its historic classrooms amidst its flowering privilege, and I was tired. Maybe Rutledge had been right, and I'd become more gargoyle than guru, hiding out here where it didn't matter who I was or what I did. My father had been an adventurer, a seeker of truths, a life-glutton. I was none of those things.

"What the hell, Chrys," I sighed.

Chrys didn't answer, but then she never did. She was a white oak, a pretty wooden centenarian that took root outside Casper Hall when both tree and hall were saplings, and the school itself was young. Around World War II faculty from the history department had named the growing tree Chrys after the Greek dryad Chrysopeleia, the nymph of a sacred oak who married a mortal man and with him founded the ancient Greek kingdom of Arcadia. *History faculty must have been as much fun at parties in the 1940s as they are now.* Still, the name caught on as these things do at places like Arcadia. I called the tree Chrys like everyone else, and sometimes talked with her when the legal pad was blank. I didn't mind that she never answered. It was nice to get the last word once in a while. Tradition claimed that kissing under her boughs brought luck to both parties. It was a theory I'd yet to test.

A slow dirge escaped from the bells in the high clock tower of Tappan Hall, the imposing administrative building that stared sternly at Casper from across the flat-stone courtyard. Tappan was the oldest and most beautiful of the buildings on campus, a four-story orgasm of the Romanesque Revival style so popular on private school campuses when it was erected a century before. Pointed minarets of red-brown brick rose from each of the four rounded corners, gray Munson slate from Canada tiled the slanting roofs, and attentive rows of fourteen-foot windows lined each smooth-mortared wall. The building's most iconic feature was the clock tower stretching an additional two stories above the main structure, piercing the sky with phallic vitality. When the bells rang out from her depths, as they did now, no one on campus could mistake the time. Even in this age of cellular phones and smart watches, many students and more faculty relied on that venerable timepiece to mark the hours of the academic day.

Tappan Hall was named for Lionel Tappan, the godfather, or perhaps midwife, of Arcadia School. During the Civil War, Colonel Tappan commanded the 2nd Maryland Regiment Cavalry in New Orleans. He left much of his left arm in Louisiana in 1864 along with the remains of his two sons, Enoch and Thomas. A widower and now childless, he bequeathed his sprawling family farm in Maryland, snug against the northern shore of the Potomac River, to the education of young men. It would take almost three decades for the old man to die, but Tappan Hall was finally built in 1889 on a central rise of the property, with majestic views of Maryland and Virginia both. A grim oil portrait of Tappan was placed in the vestibule, and there it remained. Father Lionel startled generations of students with his long forked beard, his armless left shoulder, and the searing cinders of his eyes. It was a remarkably lifelike portrait, with the crisp and unforgiving detail rendered by the photographic style of the time, and it was enormous. Another Arcadia legend held that if you were looking into the eyes of The Colonel when the bells rang in the tower, you lost a year of your life. Consequently, few lingered in the entryway near the colossal portrait, the better to avoid a chance encounter with those hellish eyes at the wrong time. Not me. I would stand there, returning Colonel Tappan's stare, questing into those soot-black eyes with my own, groping for a past well out of reach. Sometimes the bells rang. With any luck, I'd be robbed of a year vegetating in assisted living.

It was in that vestibule that Dr. Collingwood found me. It wasn't unusual to see her out of her office; Phyllis Collingwood was one of those Heads of School who considered it part of her duty to prowl the campus, seeing and being seen, distributing her regal presence to all of those in her care. In her own way, she was as impressive and unsettling a figure as the late and supposedly lethal Lionel Tappan. Well above six feet tall and impossibly slender, Dr. Collingwood moved stiffly with a slight bent to her posture, giving the impression of a towering and mildly hungry praying mantis, an image reinforced by her outsized rimless glasses. She was a gray mantis; her hair manicured steel, her skin the kind of fading charcoal you sometimes saw in older black women, skin that seemed to be tired of being black along with everything else it was tired of. Dr. Collingwood was the smartest and toughest person at Arcadia. She was also the only person on campus who knew Isaiah Moss was my father.

"Doctor Kendall," she said, her voice gravel and authority and fatigue.

Phyllis Collingwood was the only one who ever called me Doctor. I think she used it because she liked to tell Arcadia parents how many PhDs there were teaching their cossetted offspring. I was uncomfortable with the honorific myself. Not long after earning my doctorate in Literature at Boston University, I was coming back from some academic conference and had peeled my name tag off my lapel and stuck it on the binder I was carrying. The young woman sitting next to me on the plane must have noticed it, because she put her hand on my arm and asked with dewy admiration if I was a doctor. I was young and newly divorced, she was pretty and nearby, and so I said I was, which led to a couple of cocktails and promising conversation. Midway through the flight, there was some commotion a few rows away. Like some ludicrous scene from a movie, a stewardess called for a doctor to help a man who apparently was choking.

"Right here!" called my seatmate, and I managed to somehow turn red with embarrassment and white with terror at the same time. "He's a doctor!"

Heads and eyes swiveled toward me.

"Is he choking on his words?" I asked weakly.

Fortunately, an elderly cardiologist was also on the flight and was able to minister to the man who had so inconsiderately neglected to chew his food, so there were no casualties other than my pride. The look the pretty young woman gave me, of reproach and disgust, curdled in my gut. I haven't called myself "Doctor" since.

"Doctor Kendall," Dr. Collingwood repeated, "Won't you come and sit with me in my office?"

My first instinct was that either I had done something wrong or one of my students had, but the not unkindly look behind those massive glasses told me it might be something else entirely. Dr. Collingwood had a formality about her, a whiff of dignified gentility from another age. She was unfailingly polite without ever being familiar, and was my favorite of the Heads I'd worked for at Arcadia. Dr. Phyllis Collingwood wasn't ephemera. She was the opposite of ephemera. There was a solidity to her, a kind of inescapable gravity that belied her skeletal frame. She'd been poached a few years before from one of the prestigious downtown DC schools to replace Cabot Rutledge after the Regents fired him for the crime of being terrible at his job, and since then she had established herself as the most competent, intimidating head of school most of us had ever known.

Her office was spacious, airy and filled with greenery. There were dangling tendrils of ivy, snug little clusters of violets, voluble spider ferns, an improbably vast potted ficus. There weren't any family pictures in that office, because Dr. Collingwood didn't have any family that I knew of. Just plants. She had no patience for the independence of cats, so Dr. Collingwood loved her plants instead, doting on them as only as an aging chaste lesbian could. At least, some of us in the faculty believed she was a chaste lesbian. Others claimed that she wasn't chaste at all but led an active night life in Baltimore, and a few years back a rumor circulated that she had once been married to Willie Mays. I think Dr. Collingwood enjoyed letting the mystery persist, though she'd never admit it.

A pair of simple slat-backed oak chairs faced the Head's desk, and I sat in one. They were handsome enough, though hard on the cheeks. Dr. Collingwood once told the assembled faculty of Arcadia School that she didn't want anyone finding themselves too comfortable in her office. "The day a problem takes more than thirty minutes to solve is the day I retire," she said. Seventy had come and gone, and she was still on the job. Her chair, of course, was thickly cushioned and upholstered with a rich red leather. Settling behind her massive wooden desk, Dr. Collingwood placed her pointy, bony elbows on the surface, laced her long, bony fingers together, and fixed me with her inscrutable, bony gaze.

"Doctor Kendall," she said, "I am sorry for your loss."

I stared at her.

"My...loss?"

She squinted at me through her large glasses.

"Your father?"

My stomach filled up with a sudden coldness, like I'd swallowed all the ice cubes from my glass at once.

"What about my father?"

"You don't know?" she asked, tilting her regal head and looking at me with skepticism.

"Know what?" There was a pause, as though she were considering.

"I presumed you knew. Very well, then, we're in it now. Doctor Kendall, I am very sorry to say that your father passed away yesterday."

"Isaiah Moss is dead?" I asked.

It was her turn to stare at me.

"Was Isaiah Moss your father?"

"Yes."

"Then your father is dead." She made no move to reach out for my hand or offer comfort. There was nothing aloof or cold in the absent gesture; Phyllis Collingwood was simply not a woman made for casual warmth.

Isaiah Moss dead. It was as though someone had torn down the Pyramids or filled in the Grand Canyon. Some things are supposed to be eternal.

"How did you find out?" I asked.

"Twitter."

I laughed then, because it was funny. It made sense that the world knew before I did. I felt surprise, I felt loss, but I did not feel grief. Something was missing now from the world. It had been a month or two since I'd gotten a letter, and now I'd never get another one. That voice, that masterful voice, silenced forever.

"If you need a moment..."

"A moment is more than he ever gave me," I replied, and the firmness in my own voice came as something of a surprise. "Thanks for letting me know. Is there anything else?"

Dr. Collingwood shook her head slowly, quietly. I nodded, stood up, and left.

On my way out of the building, the bells rang. I could feel Colonel Tappan's eyes on my back.

~~~

Perhaps the most thoughtful thing my father ever did was to die in the late spring, when the school year was about to wrap up. It was my tenth year coaching the Arcadia Upper School girls' varsity softball team, and while my teams had never won more than they'd lost, sometimes it was close. A couple of years before, the girls had posted an almost-respectable 13-14 record. Arcadia had a strong academic standing, as well as a certain reputation in the performing arts, but athletics were an afterthought. Coaching was an assumed duty of the faculty at the school, and as the newest hire a decade before, I'd been assigned to the bottom-feeding softball team no one else wanted. That was fine with me. There were no expectations, which was where I did my best work. There was a certain pleasure to spending time outdoors in the mid-Atlantic spring, those beautiful cerulean weeks between misty winter and sweltering summer. It reminded me forcefully of my own flirtations with baseball, a long time ago when possibilities were still a thing. While the girls weren't quite winners they rarely failed to try, and I respected that. Trying and failing was the main reason I didn't really try, so to see these privileged young women doing it again and again was a source of bemused awe for me.

Our season-ending game that spring was the last thing I had to do before attending to my father's passing. The executor was handling most things, but I did have to be present at the reading of his will and I had to check in on my poor mom. She had loved the old man, with the unexamined, uncomplicated reverence of youthful infatuation. Having never lived together, never grown old together, she had never cultivated the garden of minor annoyances characteristic of long relationships, grinding unbridled passion down to a companionable mutual tolerance.

The Spartans of Arcadia uneventfully dropped that last game of our uneventful season. I don't recall the score, but it wasn't close. In the school's minibus on the way back to campus I sat behind our driver, thinking vaguely of strikeouts with runners on third base and the blisteringly good writing of my dead father. My fingers itched to hold a pen, to scrawl some rich lines about the undying nature of youth, the cyclic reinvention of spring on basepaths, sport for the sake of itself. Instead I closed my eyes and leaned my forehead against the cool glass of the dark window. *Even if I write it, who would care?*

Despite the hefty tuition at Arcadia, the minibus wasn't some ritzy charter deal with cushy captain's chairs and TV screens hanging from the ceiling. It looked like a school bus that had never gotten past puberty, the sawed-off runt of the scholastic transportation family. It wasn't even the traditional yellow, but white with rakishly angled blue and yellow stripes down the side and green vinyl bench seats. "It handles like butter," the driver said one time, "butter that rattles when it tickles sixty on the speedometer." Even well-endowed private schools have their food chains, and we were not at the top. We weren't even at the middle.

"Mister Coach Kendall?"

Odette Kieffer was one of my favorites. Teachers, like parents, will tell you that they don't have favorites, but that's pretty much bullshit. Of course we have favorites. Odette was a decent player, scrappy and tough at second base, the kind of student who excelled in the classroom because her penmanship was decipherable, and her answers were inoffensively sufficient. Unimaginative, workmanlike, good enough. Polite, well-spoken with the lilt of continental French as her first language, second clarinet in the school band. Pretty, in that way that most seventeen-year-old girls are pretty; smooth and lean and still unbroken. Odette would go far. It helped that her mother was a diplomat from Belgium or Andorra or someplace and had all the money. I think she was really my favorite because she had coined the "Mister Coach Kendall" that grew into common usage among the girls who had me in the classroom and on the softball field. How do you not like that?

"Hey." I sort of wanted to be left alone, to set aside the oppressive weight of being an adult and drown in my own unsettled thoughts, but Odette sidled next to me on the green vinyl bench in her silky warm-ups. She was almost as tall as I was, and the eye black she liked to put on before games had started to streak down her cheekbones, making her look like a KISS groupie from a generation even earlier than mine. It was dark, passing headlights suffusing the minibus interior with brief, intermittent flashes of illumination. I realized I was very tired.

"I wanted to say that I am sorry about your father."

Secrets are notoriously scarce in the insular societies of independent schools, which is why I so resolutely guarded my father's identity, even now. *Especially now.* I felt a gentle, warm pressure on my right hand where it rested on the cool vinyl. Odette had put her hand on mine. It was as smooth as you might expect. I remembered then that her mother was the ambassador to the United States from Luxembourg. I taught literature, not geography. I didn't know where the fuck Luxembourg was. But I knew where they sent you if you messed around with underage girls, and I wanted no part of it.

Even so, looking down at her young hand on mine, I was briefly paralyzed. *Oh, if I were seventeen myself.* But I wasn't. I was forty-three, rudderless, dissipated, sated on the fruit of the tree of knowledge. I was a lot of things, but I wasn't evil. I wasn't a corruptor of youth. I wasn't a Florida Congressman, for God's sake. I reached across my body with my left hand, placing it on top of hers, and looked Odette in the eye.

"Thanks," I said, a bit huskier than I intended, and then took my hands away. Slowly, not unkindly. "Odette, you're one of the good ones." It sounded stupider in my mouth than it had in my head. She looked back at me, those big brown heifer eyes, Disney character eyes, full of innocence and expectation and hurt, and I felt small. The last thing I wanted to do was hurt her. *No*, I thought, the last thing I wanted was to be hurt myself. But damaging a fawn like Odette was pretty low on my list. She looked back at me, unsure whether to be offended or confused before deciding on gently rebuffed, God love her.

"Mister Coach Kendall," she said, "I just wanted you to know you aren't alone."

"Thanks, kid." I put a gentle emphasis on that second word. Odette smiled at me, and melted back into the amorphous potentialities of the girls behind me. Bullet dodged, limp-wristed virtue confirmed, I stared out the window for the remainder of the ride. No matter what Odette said, or what Dr. Collingwood said, I was alone.

That night I jacked off vigorously, thinking of Odette.

"Masturbation," my father had once written to me in one of his letters, "is the last vestige of privacy and fantasy. Marilyn Monroe, Daisy Duck, Nancy Reagan, Mother Teresa. Fuck them all. At once. Nobody ever needs to know."

I slept like a dreamless rock.

~~~

There was no celebrity funeral for my father, no public service providing an open-air opportunity for the famous and famous-adjacent to pay homage to the dead icon, to fold themselves into black silk and wax personal about how the writing of Isaiah Moss changed their lives. "He wouldn't have wanted that," my mother said, which was ridiculous. Of course he would have wanted that. He would have wanted the world to grind to a halt with the hair-pulling and garment-rending of our collective grief, for us to cut our scalps with sharpened conch shells and wail like Polynesian widows. His passing trended on Twitter, of course, and it was there the attention-seeking glitterati could be found by his virtual graveside. #MossMemories, that sort of thing, stories of how his books changed the world. There were also the obligatory full-page obituaries in the *Times* and the *Guardian* and other papers of repute, a cover of *Newsweek*, notice taken by the grave men who read the news at night. The man himself had been cremated as per his instructions, his well-used body incinerated and deposited ash-first into a cheap metal urn. There was no granite headstone marking his life, no permanent final resting place. The earthiest of men wanted no earthly repose.

His will was specific on a few key points, and this was one. "I never once ate a worm," it read. "I see no reason that they should get to eat me. Whatever I might have been is in my books. I need no other memorial. You can find me in those pages, as alive as I ever was." You could almost hear him pause before adding "Buy your own copies. Libraries are literary whorehouses." His ashes were to be consigned to the waters of Franklin Lake in northern New Hampshire, where my father had owned a small cabin and done the bulk of his writing. He had died there, carried off by a simultaneous cardiac arrest and stroke, his heart and brain quitting in unison as if by mutual agreement. The cabin was also the extent of my inheritance. His spacious and seldom-used Upper East Side apartment in New York was to be sold, the proceeds packaged into a trust benefitting the Korean War Memorial in D.C. The rights and royalties for the published works of Isaiah Moss, valued in the hundreds of millions, were bequeathed in perpetuity to the same memorial. A bunch of dead statues got a fortune. I got a cottage.

Turns out the old man did have a sentimental side. Just not for me.

CHAPTER TWO

Did I say I don't need some armchair psychologist? Maybe, maybe not, but I have one all the same. Everyone has one in the D.C. 'burbs, like having a dentist or a lawn guy. I went to see her after the reading of my father's will. Not because I felt emotional or conflicted, but because for the most part I didn't feel anything at all. Not sad, not bereaved, not angry. Well, I was a little pissed that he wasn't leaving me a ton of money, but I mainly felt as though an old professional athlete I had rooted for as a kid had died, or a movie star from the '80s, someone I knew about rather than knew. I figured it was worth talking with Dr. Midge about whether it made me a sociopath that my father's death didn't really bother me.

Dr. Midge had a little basement office in a whitewashed brick office park in Kensington, a sleepy oak-leaf town just north of Bethesda. She was able to fit me right in, which surprised me a bit. Dr. Midge was a Teutonic stickler for schedules. You didn't waltz in five minutes late for an appointment with Dr. Midge without enduring a withering glare under impossibly-arched, impossibly-thin white eyebrows. She insisted on being called Dr. Midge because her last name, Ottoschenfelde, rolled off the tongue like a cement mixer.

"So Oscar," she said as she greeted me with her customary absence of prelude or nicety. When you paid for forty-five minutes with Dr. Midge, you got forty-five minutes. "He is dead."

Dr. Midge had a fantastic German accent. It gave the patient the impression of being analyzed by Freud himself, or else of being in a particularly unfunny episode of Hogan's Heroes. She was a tiny woman, maybe ninety pounds, of indeterminate age, and always wrapped in these absurd crocheted afghans. I never understood how a blanket that was mostly holes could keep you warm. She would clutch at the corners of the thing like it was a prayer shawl while she listened, sometimes a chalky little hand snaking out to jot down a note on her pad. It always made me self-conscious when she did that. *Had I just said something important? Was the rest of what I said not important? Had she just remembered something for her grocery list?* I noticed that without fail, she used cheap ballpoint pens, clicking logo-imprinted leave-behinds by pharmaceutical salesmen.

"I'm not sad," I said, legs crossed and hands folded casually. I wore jeans to our sessions, comfortable and unserious. "How can I miss someone I don't know?"

She looked back at me, beady little brown eyes, unjudgmental, vaguely bored.

"Maybe it's because you never knew him that you're upset?"

"I'm not upset." That was the truth. I wasn't upset. My father's death had left me curiously devoid of grief. "That's what's bothering me. Shouldn't I be?"

"Should." Dr. Midge tugged at her afghan. "Oscar, people come in here all time asking what they should do, how they should feel. As though I have the answer key to the test."

"I didn't know there would be a test." I gave my slyest smirk, but Dr. Midge was impervious to charm. I wondered what she'd been like as a young woman. She'd probably lost a husband when Caesar pacified the Germanic tribes and was still bitter.

"There is always a test," she replied. "Life is a testing. Not the same for everyone, of course." She shivered. It was June in Maryland, and the heat was on in her virtually featureless little office, and yet she shivered, drawing the afghan tighter about her spindly frame. "What is your test, Oscar? How can you hope to find answers when you don't even know the questions?"

"I just asked a question," I said with a touch of exasperation. Dr. Midge could be quiet for long stretches, seeming as though she wasn't even paying attention, and then once in a while she would come to life and release a torrent of accumulated words.

"You weren't seeking answers, you were seeking reassurance. *Should.* This word, *should.* It is a hopeless quest for confirmation. It places the burden of evaluation on others. It is an abdication of agency. I cannot tell you what you should feel, what you should do, who you should be. These are questions for you to ask yourself, not me. And not your father."

It was a waste of forty-five minutes and eighty bucks. I'd have been better off going to the movies.

~~~

I drove to New Hampshire from Maryland at the end of June, the early summer sun warming the asphalt miles of interstates 95 and 84 and 91 and 95 again. I listened to Billy Joel, the early Cold Spring Harbor stuff, along with some Don Henley and Bon Jovi. A child of the 1980s, my musical tastes never made it much past 1991. One moment there were songwriters I understood and could make sense of, and then out of nowhere (Seattle, I guess, which is pretty much nowhere – who plays football at 10 in the morning?), Nirvana and Pearl Jam showed up. Suddenly affluent suburban white kids were unhappy, kids who had been mindlessly content with the vacuous yodeling of Poison or Quiet Riot a few months before. Now, everything sucked, and rebellion against...well, against something, was back in vogue. Isaiah Moss, unpredictable as ever, had agreed with them.

"If you had plastic for a front lawn and nothing but debt and decline to look forward to, you'd be pissed too," he had written. "I would be depressed if all I had coming to me was the 21st century. Fucking minivans."

The music my students listen to now, the inane, overproduced, largely talentless made-for-TV shit, reminds me powerfully of my own youth and gives me faith in the future. When you're sixteen you should be listening to music about girls and cars, not pretend-angst and faux-consciousness. Music is for driving or dancing or fucking, not pouting.

So the sun shone down with egg-yolk indifference and I drove, listening to the musical equivalent of Novocain and reveling in my own semi-consciousness. There's really no other way to survive the stale boredom of New Jersey and Connecticut. My father rode next to me in the front seat, the unremarkable metal urn held firmly and conscientiously in the passenger seat by the lap belt. *Father and son road trip.* Those nine hours in my Hyundai increased the total time we'd spent together by eight hours. He was uncharacteristically quiet.

When you cross the state line into New Hampshire, not a whole lot changes other than a sudden and brief spasm of shops offering duty-free tobacco products and fireworks, catering to the tax-oppressed denizens of the People's Republic of Massachusetts. I was unsympathetic to their plight. Good schools and good health care and paved roads. *Yeah, you guys have it tough.* Other than the merchants of death along the border, southern New Hampshire is pretty much still Massachusetts for thirty or forty miles, prosperous towns with smug colonial architecture and a lifetime supply of road work. Once you get past Concord or Rochester you start to penetrate the real guts of the state, a place that loves to talk Libertarian and then vote with their Democratic hearts or Republican wallets like everywhere else. I drove Route 16 north, also called the Spalding Turnpike by the locals. It was apparently named after a pair of brothers who each took a turn as the state's governor back in the early decades of the 20th century, which is one of the most New Hampshire things I've ever heard.

I turned off the 'pike when prompted by the map on my cell phone, and promptly found myself on a two-lane country road, driving past tractor supply stores, shuttered gas stations, and donut shops. At one point there was a pop-up tent sheltering one sizable, forlorn-looking woman with a handmade sign advertising fresh strawberries and corn. The forested granite hills combined with my musical selections to trigger a sustained wave of nostalgia. Franklin Lake was

Joe Pace

not all that far east of Dartmouth College, my undergraduate alma mater, where I'd spent four years studying literature, hiding from every tweed-clad English professor that I was the sole son and heir to the towering talent that was Isaiah Moss. When he gave a guest lecture at Dartmouth during my senior year, my father made no effort to see me. I extended him the same courtesy and avoided the event.

A right, a left, and a right later I was on a rutted, unpaved road and my electronic directions had thrown up their hands at the lack of satellite guidance. I proceeded at a crawling turtle's sprint, worried about finding my destination and about my Hyundai's undercarriage. Out my passenger window I could see a few flashes of sparkling blue-white away through the trees and down the sloping hillside, my first glimpses of Franklin Lake. Occasional buildings dotted the roadside, mostly dowdy gray or brown structures that looked like three-season rentals. After one particularly nerve-testing curve, the trees fell away and I was rewarded with a spectacular vista of rippling blue, but only for a moment before it was swallowed up again.

I had never been to my father's cabin, but I knew what it looked like. A couple of decades prior, the *New Yorker* had published an interview with Isaiah Moss, one of those frothy, overwrought puff pieces that get written about gods. The article had featured a black-and-white photograph of the artiste himself standing, arms crossed over an ample midsection, scowling darkly into the lens. It had become an iconic shot, the image many magazines and newspapers chose to use with their retrospectives and hagiographies when the old man died. It was either that or the much-older picture of him as a young man barefoot on some Mediterranean beach in khakis and a crisp collared shirt completely unbuttoned over his much-younger and less fleshy midsection, Ray-Bans and coal-grey wool fedora over the same scowl. 1960s Isaiah Moss and 1980s Isaiah Moss were two different animals, one a jet-set literary sex symbol, the other a thickening reclusive genius. Think Connery as Bond in Dr.

30

No compared to Never Say Never Again. Or, if you prefer, Young Elvis and Fat Elvis.

Behind him in the Fat Elvis photograph, through a screen of anorexic pines, the cabin perched on a narrow outcrop thrusting into one of the many coves of Franklin Lake. Armored in weather-worn cedar shakes siding, the cabin had no windows facing the dirt access road, a defensible bunker of a retreat. Seldom an adherent to any kind of convention, my father had observed it here, nailing the cabin's name to those pines on a hand-painted wooden sign, clearly visible in that famous picture. Where mere mortals would hang signs proudly and lovingly declaring their waterfront property to be "Loon's Landing" or "Lakeview", this sign, in spiky black script, read "The Scrotum".

"All great creations begin there," he had told that *New Yorker* writer, probably some open-mouthed young Manhattanite he had introduced to more than one scrotum that evening. Not a few of his later letters to me began "Here I am in the Ball Sack." Isaiah Moss had been an vulgar and venal creature, evidence that while talentless assholes are just assholes, talented assholes become eccentrics.

After what felt like an eternity of creeping along, I found it.

I parked in front of the cabin for the first time, prepared for awkward tension, for the unwelcome of my father's baleful spirit, but my first sensation as I stepped out of the car was one of peace. If ever a man lived so that he had no need to linger after his death it was Isaiah Moss. After all, he never did the same thing twice. That peace lasted long enough for my second foot to touch the sand-and-gravel driveway before I heard a voice, equal parts cheese grater and dying roses, shatter the silence.

"You can't park there, young man," it wailed, a physical thing. Her Down East accent was spectacular, transforming terminal Rs into an absurdly ascendant "yah" and adding entire creaking syllables to words that had no place to put them. "That's private property." The owner of the voice came into view, a wizened hobbit of a woman, perhaps an inch shy of five feet tall, and belt-thin. At my own six-foot and change, I towered over her. I would have put her age at a hundred and ten, except she moved like one of the girls on my softball teams, lithe and confident. She was clearly a home-grown New Englander, the throaty scrape of her accent made that abundantly evident as she stomped through those emaciated trees in hiking boots, tattered beige shorts, and a loose gray sweatshirt under which old breasts moved beneath with elderly freedom. She looked like one of the nearby pines had sprung reluctantly to life, a gnarled animate root, her skin corrugated and brown beneath a riot of white fluffy hair like a dying dandelion.

"It's okay," I called. I realized who this was. "You must be Ruby Pierce." My father's letters had mentioned her with some frequency, usually in the context of "afternoon sex with the Pierce widow." Lovely grist for a ten-year old boy. My mother, bless her heart, had never thought to preview those letters, or else she'd tried and gave up when she failed to understand much of what was in them. I made a half-hearted attempt to picture their coupling but without much effort or enthusiasm. Hearing her own name brought Ruby up short, and she blinked at me twice from behind tortoise-shell horn-rimmed glasses.

"How d'ya know who I am, boy?"

"I'm Oscar Kendall, ma'am." I extended a hand. "I'm Isaiah Moss's only child." Pause. "That I know of." It was an old joke, one I'd relied on at need. She didn't laugh, didn't smile, didn't shake my hand. I let it drop to my side. Maybe she didn't have it in her to bully that boiled leather face into anything other than a resting scowl. Instead she leveled a glare at me, beady little eyes behind those ludicrous glasses, her head at a tilt that suggested she either hadn't heard me or hadn't believed me.

"Never heard of you," said the Widow Pierce at last. "He never talked about you."

"He never mentioned you, either," I lied. "But I have a key, and a deed, so..." I spread my hands in the universal gesture of what-can-you-do. What I really wanted to do was produce a different universal gesture so the toady little creature would leave me alone. I wanted to go inside, into my father's private retreat, and I had no interest in doing so in the company of this Yankee hag. I wanted to be alone. Alone was when I was at my best.

The sun shone down with the beatific warmth of late June while she considered my words. Her puckered, probably toothless mouth worked silently like a fish on a dock sucking for oxygen that wouldn't come. After what seemed a cordial stretch of patience, I nodded at her with the kind of indulgent smile you reserve for the very stupid or the very old.

"It was nice to meet you," I lied again. "I – am – going – inside – now." I pointed slowly at myself and then at the cabin to be perfectly clear who the I was and where the inside was. "And I'm sorry," I added. "But this is private property." Leaving the Widow Pierce behind to wrestle with that, I tucked the urn of my father's ashes under my arm and navigated the stone steps down to the cabin. There was no cultivated greenery, no flowers, no nod to civilization, just ferns and moss and pine needles. Whatever grew here grew wild and unintentional. When the executor of my father's estate, his literary agent Ginger Greene, handed over the key to the cabin, the childish part of me had been hoping for something unusual and gothic. Instead, it was simply a plain metal key, the kind you get at the hardware store when you make duplicates for the cleaners. It had been given to me at the reading of his will, along with the deed, when Ginger told me the cabin and its contents were the extent of my inheritance. There was no mortgage to inherit. Isaiah Moss hadn't believed in debt with the hardened zeal of a man whose monthly royalty checks could buy a major league center fielder or jump-start the economy of a small island nation.

The front door was an unembellished beige rectangle on cast iron hinges. Nearby was the sole exception to the uncultivated dooryard, a stubby young lilac bush maybe three feet tall, done flowering for the year. It stood there squat and sheepish and yet defiant, a leafy toddler unready for its nap. The door rewarded me with an appreciative groan as I turned the key in the heavy lock and swung it open. Inside, it was surprisingly mundane. I walked with tentative care into the short hallway, the walls of raw pine narrow enough that I could reach out and touch both sides while my elbows were still bent. There were doors on either wall which at a cursory glance led to a bedroom and a bathroom. The hall opened onto a single modest space with an overstuffed couch and knotty coffee table, no decoration other than a threadbare woven tapestry of a big moose knee-deep in water above the couch. A kitchenette with cramped dining nook huddled off to the left, and to the right loomed a big fieldstone fireplace, mortared with a gray granite slab of a mantel, black-iron fixtures in the cold hearth. A plywood crib sat nearby, half-full of split white oak and an under-construction spiderweb.

The far wall was entirely swallowed up by glass; a huge bay window to the right and a sliding door to the left. Beyond was a spreading panorama of sky and water, New Hampshire early summer in its near glory, pregnant and ready to deliver. But the view wasn't what made my heart trip over its own rhythm and then sprint into a staccato gallop. Looking out the window was a sturdy desk, and on it, a typewriter.

His typewriter.

My mouth went dry as I approached it. I was a pilgrim on holy ground, past the vestibule and into the inner sanctum, and now the holy relic itself was in sight. The crown of thorns, the chains of St. Paul, the head of John the Baptist. It was black and heavy, with its own gravity independent of the earth's pull beneath us. I knew he had shunned computers and word processors, because he had said as much in one of his letters to me, a drunken screed against the unnatural sin of words made of light instead of ink. "Imaginary idols," he called them, "golden calves, false gods." Isaiah Moss was a typewriter man, a devotee of the physical act of writing, of the tactile forming of words on a page through the violent act of striking a key. He never wrote with pens if he could help it, avoiding what he called the "sloppy fermentation of the idea". My father did not sketch; he went right for the paintbrush. This typewriter, *his* typewriter, dated from his incarnation as a journalist after Korea, a newspaperman in the mid-fifties, the last of the fedora-and-tie crowd before Kennedy came around with his open collars and uncapped coiffure. His days with the Chicago Tribune had numbered in the hundreds, covering Mayor Daley's city hall machine, drinking with cops and gangsters, precinct-captains and vote-buyers. Within two years he had written *Whistle Stop*, his first bestselling novel, and he quit the newspaper business to become a world-famous writer. He was twenty-five years old. God, I hated him.

He had written it on this typewriter, this gorgeous, monstrous antique, and he never abandoned her. "She never cheated on me," he wrote me once. "Never betrayed me. So I never cheated on her." The one true love of my father's life, his monogamous and faithful partner, had been a 1948 Remington Rand Deluxe 5. He used it and maintained it and repaired it for over half a century, and together they had spawned five iconic novels (and several others nearly as Olympian), dozens of short stories, and a series of rambling, intimidating letters to his only fleshly issue.

The keys stood independent of each other, poised and erect, round keys suspended at the end of their levers, each embossed with a letter or number or punctuation mark in workmanlike black script against a field of pearly white. Years of fervent use had worn the keypads, rounding their edges like the sea softens broken glass. I reached out a hand to touch them, and then shied away. I wasn't ready, not yet. It was too intimate. This after all, was the receptacle of the love and fidelity my father had been unwilling or unable to muster for my mother. Or for me.

"He's not coming back," I murmured at it in consoling mockery.

It was then I noticed the paper.

A sheet of white bond paper still hugged the graceful curve of the platen, forever waiting for the touch of genius that would never come. There were words on it too, black agate letters. He had been working on something when his body fell apart like the car at the end of the Blues Brothers. Ginger Greene had told me that he'd been found by the woman next door. *Ruby,* I thought. It must have been Ruby who found him dead at his work, Ruby who called the ambulance that took him on a slow ride to the hospital in Laconia, Ruby who had left his effects untouched. *Maybe there had been more than afternoon sex with the widow Pierce.*

I glanced at it but couldn't make sense of it. The words were jumbled and impenetrable, the unfortunate love child of a confused Joyce and a bag of Scrabble tiles. That singular brain, that unique and brilliant voice, had been reduced to gibberish at the end. The last word that could be clearly made out was "alone".

The Remington wasn't alone. A half-full bottle of Jim Beam stood alongside, cap off, accompanied by a sturdy little highball glass. An ashtray, white ceramic with painted palm trees and a dead cigar. It was a wonder the bastard had lived to nearly ninety. On the other side of the typewriter, sitting in a tidy stack on that oaken desk, was a ream of paper. Had he just been sitting down to start another bestseller, a valedictory entry in the Canon of St. Isaiah? No, there were words on the top sheet. *The Last Sane Man*, it read, all in capital letters, graven like commandments on stone. I deposited the urn on the desk next to the Jim Beam where my father would feel at home, and lifted the page. The one beneath it was full of text, as was the next, and the next. Holding my breath, I picked up the entire stack and riffled through it. Every page was covered in type, words making sentences making paragraphs, gathering into chapters. This was a complete manuscript. This was a complete, unpublished, unknown Isaiah Moss manuscript.

"Holy shit," I breathed.

I picked it up and began to read. After six pages, I took the bottle of bourbon, a fresh glass from the kitchen, and sat down on the orange-and-rust floral couch. This wasn't simply another book by Isaiah Moss. This was his best book. His magnum opus.

And nobody knew about it but me.

~~~

The novel widely regarded as second-best among the Isaiah Moss portfolio was *Holding Your Breath*, though there were those who debated it should be number one, or at least 1A, among the curious souls who debated such things. Yes, I know you've read it. Everyone has. Everyone claims to have, anyway. Usually that means they read just enough to pass junior year English in high school. At any rate, there is a passage in it where he describes the cry of a loon at night as "the death of childhood made music". Yes, he wrote like that, equal parts brilliance and pretention, making him beloved of the literati. I had never heard a loon before that first night at his cabin, and when I did hear it, it sounded exactly like the death of childhood made music. I had no idea what time it was, but it was late and dark, a lambent knife of moonlight stabbing across the surface of the lake, transforming tall pines and spruces on the far shoreline into malevolent purple sentinels, jagged and hungry. I set the typewritten page I'd been reading atop its fellows, gently, almost reverently. When handling holy relics, one exercises care. A cigar I'd begun smoldered in an ashtray next to the now mostly empty bottle of Jim Beam. I took both and went out onto the deck.

The moon wasn't alone up there. The welkin was a carpet of stars, a full shaker of salt strewn across a black velvet cloth. I stared upward until my neck ached, feeling smaller than ever. It was majestic, it was eternal and humbling, and yet even that vast galactic panoply paled alongside what I was reading. I brought the bottle to my trembling lips – his bottle, his sauce – and chased it with a long drag from that excellent cigar. It was cold out on the deck, cold in the echo of the loons, cold under that heavy blanket of exploding helium and hydrogen, but I had fire in my hand and fire in my belly, both of which I'd stolen from him. *Stolen? Or inherited?* If anyone deserved this inheritance, it was me. But how much more could I take? And would he care? Even if he weren't ashes in a jar, even if he knew, would he care?

It wouldn't be honest, to claim his work. But it would be smart. *Which of those did Isaiah Moss respect more? I* thought I knew that answer to that question.

The right thing to do would be to contact his agent and publish it posthumously under his name. Maybe fiddle with it just enough that I could justify to myself a tithe of credit. *The Last Sane Man*, by Isaiah Moss and Oscar Kendall. But that would be like fucking with a Michelangelo fresco, or a Mozart symphony. And I had no interest in being Tolkien's kid, squeezing the last monetary ounces out of my father's legacy, inexorably eroding it from iconic to mediocre. I'd just screw it up. It was perfect as it was.

"You asshole!" I shouted into the dark, and threw the empty bottle as far as I could out over the lake. I heard it hit the surface with a hollow and deeply unsatisfying plunk. Not as far as I might have hoped, but far enough.

Right had never been the foremost concern of Isaiah Moss. He screwed and screwed over plenty of people during his time on this Earth. As far as I could tell, he'd never been a victim himself. It would serve him right to have his finest work credited to someone else. It would serve him right if the son he wasn't proud of and didn't love robbed him while his ashes still cooled and his death still trended on Twitter. It was something Isaiah Moss would do.

Hell, I thought, *maybe he* meant *me to find it.*

Maybe the cabin wasn't my only inheritance after all.

Maybe the cabin was just the gift wrapping.

~~~

When the sun came up over the lake, I hadn't slept. I had read and read and smoked and drank and read, but I hadn't slept. I was hungry more than tired, my head a miasmic fog of cigar smoke, bourbon, and indecision. *Food,* I thought, and shuffled into the modest kitchen. Each step in his footsteps, each step tracing the pattern of his brilliance and his dissolution.

The cabin had surprised me with its tidiness. I had expected some outer expression of my father's inherent rejection of order – stacks of books and newspapers, overflowing trash, stray socks, chaos. But the place had been straightened up for the most part; the bed was made, no dirty dishes in the sink. Even the groceries in the fridge weren't much past their expiration dates. Some had even outlasted the man who had bought them. Isaiah Moss had been more fastidious than I'd previously believed, or else he'd had a guardian angel.

I found a can of vegetable soup in the pantry and heated it up on the stove. I ate on the ramshackle deck overlooking the lake, and watched the sun climb. The carrots and celery had the same wet-cardboard consistency I remembered from childhood, the same comforting mediocrity that enveloped and encouraged without exciting the tongue. It was to eating what most prose was to Isaiah Moss. Then I went inside and called my mother. There was no cell service at the lake, so I used the cabin phone, an ancient rotary model, plugged into the wall and sitting on a wooden end table. It was very orange. When I picked up the receiver, I felt like I was about to call Adam West and warn him that the Riddler was at it again in Gotham. The sound of the dial spinning was as comforting, as evocative of childhood, as the soup.

"Does it smell like him?" she asked, after we exchanged the usual pleasantries.

I didn't want to tell my mother that I had no recollection of any odor related to my father. That said, if he had smelled like anything, it would probably have been the mix of old man and brown whiskey all around me. White sleeveless tee shirt, steel-gray underarm hair, hazy regret. Bereft of my father's gift for lying to women, I told her as much. There was a brief pause on the other end of the line followed by the hint of a sniffle. *Was she crying? Had she actually loved that old bastard?* Probably. She was a credulous and sentimental creature, my mother.

I briefly considered telling her about the manuscript, asking for her advice, but it didn't take long to remember that any confidence I'd ever had in her critical thinking skills had evaporated in seventh grade. I had gone to her with concerns the afternoon before my first real date, a trip to the movies with Colleen Winters. Colleen was this sweet little thing with long braids and a smile full of braces. When I told my mother I was nervous about kissing her, she laughed and told me to wear clean underwear, and if Colleen wanted to sleep with me, not to refuse her. I was fourteen. While I suspected my mother was a bit dotty, that confirmed it, and I never sought her advice again. Though to be honest, I did wear clean underwear for that date. Not that it mattered. We went to see the last Indiana Jones movie and I remember it vividly because I saw every second of it. I don't think Colleen and I looked at each other once the entire time, lodged in the molasses of adolescent hormonal paralysis. In high school, Colleen became a cheerleader, shaped precisely as they had in mind when they designed the skirt-and-snug sweater uniforms, and more than once I regretted my inaction at the theater. I'm sure Indy would have made a move.

"I think I'm going to stick around here for a bit," I told my mother. "Yeah. Something about the place makes me want to write."

"That's nice, honey," she replied, and we said goodbye. If I had said, "I think I'm going to drop some acid and blow my brains out with a twelve gauge," she would have said the same thing. She'd been saying "that's nice, honey" my entire life. I had stopped showing her my writing by middle school because invariably I was honey and it was nice. I planned to have it engraved on her tombstone someday: Here lies Peggy Kendall, Loving Mother, It Was Nice Honey. I had told her the truth – I usually told my mother the truth, because she was so unfailingly accepting, a truly unconditionally affectionate parent. It was like having the proverbial angel and demon on either shoulder, one heaping banal praise on mediocrity, the other reminding me how repulsive that mediocrity was. My mother's bottomless hugs, my father's impossible example. I loved my mother, but I didn't really respect her. There just wasn't anything there for a person to hang their respect on. I mean, she'd been beautiful as a young woman, but physical beauty is shit luck. It's not like she followed some strict fitness regime or applied cosmetics with advanced skill or made sure she ate right. She was just naturally pretty, and that wasn't something you could give her credit for. If she'd been a talented actress or had a work ethic she might have parlayed her looks into something meaningful, but I guess that was the difference between my mother and my father. Peggy Kendall had been given beauty by God or nature or the genetic lottery and did nothing with it. Isaiah Moss had been endowed as a natural storyteller, and he spent his entire life squeezing every ounce out of his gift. That, I respected.

I hadn't lied to my mom this time either. I did feel like writing, in a way I hadn't for a long time. The yellow legal pads had been reproachfully blank for months, and had begun to wonder if I'd said everything I had to say. Reading my father's manuscript was torture; it was always torture reading his stuff, making me want to write and write and yet never write again, all at once. I was still agonizing over what to do with the book – among other things, it was a gold mine – but I had tabled that in my mind. At the moment I felt words inside me again, unbidden, an insistent, building throb like a joyful toothache. And so I wrote, but not on legal pads, and not with a blue pen.

The first time I sat at my father's desk and fed a piece of his paper into his Remington, I felt an electric thrill leavened with a twinge of silliness. It was the sort of cliché he would never have thought to write, a Hallmark television movie of a moment that would have left him raising one of those well-bristled eyebrows and deriding trite predictability. And yet the words came, my restless fingers craving the cold metal of his black-and-white typewriter keys.

"I'm coming for you, old man," I said, as I laid my hands on the love of his life and began to pound away.

Moss

CHAPTER THREE

A routine found me. I'd write until two or three in the morning, racing my father's shadow, reveling in the torrent of words that came hot and fast. It was unfamiliar and giddy. I'd shut my eyes then, eyes bleary from liquor and my own unexpected genius, but even in sleep the words wouldn't leave me alone, prodding me awake with the sun like an overeager morning lover. I'd wake and scribble in a pad by my bedside. I'd chew words with my coffee. While I showered, while I ate, while I stared at the bathroom mirror with toothbrush in hand, the words came and came. This was inspiration like I had never experienced. Calliope's divine kiss, or something like that. Whatever it was, the bourbon or the muse or my father's antique Remington, I was writing. And I knew it was the best work I'd ever done.

By mid-morning each day I would wander out onto that rickety porch, exhausted and exhilarated, clinging with one hand to a fresh cup of joe and with the other to the weather-beaten railing. The porch listed hard to starboard, away from the cabin, sloping gently but inexorably down toward the shoreline. Once presumably bright red, the two-by-six decking was a splintery pale pink with a single gunmetal-gray chair attached to the rail by a length of rusty steel chain so it wouldn't slide. I'd sit there for a while, drinking my coffee and watching the sun dapple the lake's surface. The cabin was in a modest cove, and there was less traffic here than in the main waters of Franklin Lake. Kids would go wailing past out in the center of the lake, towed on skis or tubes, or else cruising on their jet skis, but seldom ventured into the cove itself. Sometimes there would be a boat – a couple of guys fishing, or one of those party barges with a passel of white-haired retirees on board (a "box of Q-tips" Isaiah Moss once named them in a letter) – but it was usually quiet.

On the second of July, a Saturday, I sat in that chair with my coffee after a torrid night of vomiting words onto the page. Morning was when the sun soaked the cove, drenching it with heat and light, transforming the water into a sheet of diamonds, and so I sat there in boxer shorts and a bathrobe, warming myself like a turtle on a log. New England weather has a reputation for fickleness, but it had gotten the memo that June was over. There was a newly sharp prickle to the heat, and a bead of sweat formed at my hairline and rolled down my stubbly cheek. I hadn't shaved since coming to the cabin and was taking the opportunity to wallow in my own unkempt filth. The words didn't care about my whiskers or my gamey smell. They just kept coming.

A splash came from the lake nearby, too loud to have been a jumping fish. I stood up and shuffled to the edge of the deck to get a better look. A small island guarded the mouth of the cove, a rocky hump clustered with stately, judgmental pines. High up in one of these trees someone had tied a rope, and periodically college kids drunk on shitty beer or high school kids drunk on each other would visit the spot, climb as high as they could manage, swing out over the lake, and drop into the water from varying heights. Their laughter and shouts and splashes could be heard clearly across the hundred yards between the swing and the cabin, the soundtrack of a young summer. My father, I had noticed, owned excellent binoculars. Not the cheap plastic kind for the dilettante birdwatcher, but a sturdy steel set that a military sniper might use. My third afternoon at the cabin was the first time I noticed the rope-swingers. I trained my father's binoculars on them, out of idle curiosity, and was stunned at the power of the instrument. I might as well have been among the armada of teenage canoes. The lithe, unspoiled bodies of twentyish kids still too young to know what beer and pizza do to the flesh cavorted a magnified arm's length away. It was readily apparent why Isaiah Moss possessed such powerful binoculars. Young women wore swimsuits that had been designed to cover the things that wanted covering, if only just, but the scanty fabric was hard-pressed to handle the job, especially when hitting the water at high speed from the swing.

As ever, my father was a pervert. I thought of him standing on that same deck, watching the girls in the artful poses they struck, never aware they were being watched in clandestine fashion by the skeevy old author of the book their freshman American Lit professor had assigned them. I put the binoculars aside with a sigh. I thought about Odette Kieffer and how Isaiah Moss would almost certainly have handled that situation very differently. For a heartbeat I felt superior to my father, though I suppose simply not being monstrous is a fairly low bar to clear.

The splash I heard this morning was much closer than the rope swing, and I didn't need the sniper binoculars to know it had come from next door. The Scrotum's property slanted steeply down to the lake, a set of switchback cement stairs descending the slope to the waterline. It was much less hilly on the Widow Pierce's abutting property. A concrete patio behind the cottage connected to an ancient wooden deck jutting out into the water like a frail finger, and just off the end of this pier concentric ripples were subsiding where someone had gone into the water. I tried to imagine the old woman I had met upon my arrival diving in for a bracing dip, and against my will my brain conjured up images of Ruby Pierce in one of the skimpy bikinis the rope swing girls wore.

Emerging from the water a moment later was a much different figure than either the sagging glory of my elderly neighbor or the fresh ripeness of the college girls across the cove. I suppose in retrospect this is the part of the narrative where I'm supposed to wax rhapsodic about how the moment compared to Titian's Venus Anadyomene, rising from the waters and wringing her hair, or Bottecelli's version with the big scallop shell. But she wasn't nude. And she didn't have any legs.

She used her arms to haul herself backward out of the water, leaning against each step of an aluminum ladder that hung from the side of the dock. She was gasping a bit, though from the exertion or from the briskness of the early summer lake water I couldn't tell. Her swimsuit was a utilitarian one piece, athletic and black and sleek, cut high over the hips and covering the entire torso, including little half-sleeves over the arms. This was a performance suit, not a suit for a performance. Even with the sleeves I could see the toned musculature of the arms, flexing as she finished her ascent of the ladder and moved to sit on the sun-baked dock. I was struck by her evident fitness, by the grace of her clearly practiced movements, and by the absence of both legs from just above the knee. As I watched her, she picked up a nearby towel – blue, with orange starfish and green seahorses – and rubbed dry the spiky blond hair of her head. She coughed, loudly, put one index finger alongside her long nose, and blew an impressive snot-rocket into the water.

"Well," she said in a loud voice that seemed even louder in the openness of the lakefront. "The writer's son." She draped the starfish-and-seahorse towel over her rugged shoulders and leaned back, soaking in the yellow rays that descended in unhurried languor. "Are you going to say hello, or are you just going to watch?" Her smile was crooked, higher on one side than the other, muddy hazel eyes flashing with it. "There's a pair of binoculars up there somewhere if you're really shy."

"Hello," I said, because nothing else came to mind.

"If you come, bring beers."

"It's nine in the morning."

"It's dinnertime in Kabul. Your old man would have been down here half an hour ago with longnecks. They're in a fridge in the cellar."

She threw her head back, eyes closed. I went inside, put on a pair of mesh shorts and a gray Arcadia School hoops t-shirt, and went into the basement. I'd explored the cabin over the past few days, including the cobwebbed cellar. It was a dank little dungeon, full of rusty tools and a huge, cold, cast-iron All-Nighter woodstove. There weren't any water skis or fishing poles or other watersports gear you might expect at a lakefront cabin. Isaiah Moss wasn't much for playthings. As a little boy I wrote to him at my mother's suggestion, asking for some toys for Christmas. He sent me back a dictionary. On the inside cover he had scrawled, "Here are all the toys you need." I think I was five. Yes, I still have the dictionary.

I was already aware of the refrigerator, but I found it vaguely galling and unsettling that the woman next door knew about it too. And that she'd evidently had some kind of relationship with my father, that she had been Isaiah Moss's drinking buddy. There was a bucket on the floor nearby – not a brightly-colored plastic one that a child might use to carry sand, but a dull silver metal one that a pervy old writer might use to bring beer to a much younger neighbor. I loaded it up with three green Heinekens and three brown Stellas. I had no idea what this woman liked to drink.

A little dirt path led from the bottom of the steep steps of the Scrotum to the Pierce property next door, edged by unkempt blueberry bushes and moss-capped stones. There was a little stream between the properties, running down from the hills across the access road and through a culvert before blissfully gurgling under a rickety old wooden footbridge. It rocked unsteadily under my weight, nearly sending me in for my own swim.

She opened her eyes when I arrived, beer pail in hand. She took one of the Heinekens. I offered an old bottle-opener I'd thought to bring, but she shook her head. Using the edge of the dock, she pried the cap off in a single fluid motion that suggested it wasn't her first time.

"You knew my father?" I asked, watching the pale cap sink slowly until it came to rest on the bottom of the lake, an uninviting rug of pine-needle muck. The cap showed white and green and bold against the black carpet.

"Knew him? A little. He liked to watch me swim. We'd drink on the dock and he'd suggest that I do it naked. The swimming and the drinking both." She drank some of her beer. Beads of sweat ran down the glass of the green bottle, and the bare skin of her neck and arms. Her flesh was drumhead taut across the lean muscles of her body, and there was a small green tattoo behind her left ear, a bird in a cage. The door to the cage was open, but the bird remained inside. Her face was angular, sharp, striking.

"Did you?" I asked. She didn't answer, and her face gave nothing away.

"I'm May," she said.

"Like the month," I replied, fingering the peeling label on my own unopened bottle. I could drink with the best of them, but beer wasn't my favorite, and neither was pounding one in the morning. "I'm Oscar."

"Like the Grouch." She smiled then, with her mouth closed, and looked at me. It was an appraising look, one that betrayed none of the results of the appraisal.

"Your dad was a weird dude," she said eventually, finishing her bottle. She stared at it briefly, with the same kind of skeptically bored inspection she'd subjected me to. Then, with a casual explosive grace she lobbed the bottle out over the water. It was a fair toss, halfway to the rope swing, and the resulting splash was farther than I knew I could manage. I just kept picking at the label on my bottle while May took another Heineken from the bucket.

"Ruby is my grandmother," she said. I just let her talk. I had learned from my years in the classroom that certain people are allergic to silence and will chatter to fill it almost compulsively. Another bottlecap floated to the lake bottom. I wondered vaguely how many were down there. "She's been up here forever. I used to come with my aunt when I was a kid. Grew up here as much as anywhere, actually. Used to climb that tree and go flying off that rope swing." She stared at it, and the ambivalence was gone from her face, replaced with a hard cold fury. "One time, when I was sixteen, Danny O'Halloran from the next cove over dared me to swim across the lake and back. Damn near died. Gram picked me up in a canoe." She shaded her eyes from the morning sun with a long-fingered hand, looked at me again, and the ambivalence had returned. "I can hear you up there, all fucking hours of the night, clickety clack, clickety clack. You a writer like your old man?"

"I'm writing," I replied. "Hell, everyone's a writer." Every bartender and housewife is working on a novel, it seems, and there's nothing more boring than listening to them drone on about their precious story and why it isn't finished yet. Amateur authors usually won't shut up, but I never discussed my work. It felt like a betrayal of intimacy. "But there's nobody like my old man." I thought it was a clever response, witty, true, implying that I knew him better than she did. For some reason I felt the absurd dueling needs to both impress her and to mark my territory. I had started to feel like I was on sober duty at a fraternity house on Friday night, so I popped my Stella with the flimsy metal opener like a chump and took a pull, remembering immediately why beer wasn't my favorite.

"He was a weird dude," she said again. "I'd extend my condolences, but he was what, a hundred years old? And it's not like you two were close." The flex of her lithe arm, another bottle arcing to the middle of the cove. Like with the caps, I wondered vaguely how many bottles the lake had swallowed, how many dead soldiers this odd woman had committed to the depths. "Plus, sweet cabin, right?" She opened a third Heineken as deftly as she had neutered my attempt to lay claim to my father. *Saw through me like a ghost.* I drank a little more of the warming beer and thought about going back to the cabin for the bourbon. Instead, I sat down on the pier, not too close, maybe six cautious feet away, and shrugged.

"I don't think he was close to anybody," I said. "Plus, sweet cabin."

May laughed, and it was a surprisingly feminine, warm sound. I had expected something harder, a husky bark, but instead it was lovely and captivating. She had very white teeth and the top front two overlapped, just a little. It occurred to me that other than my mother, I had never really talked about my father with someone else who had known him, and my mother didn't really count. She always just told the same story, about how they met in Los Angeles back in the seventies. When I was a kid I thought it was her favorite story about my father. As I grew up, I came to realize it was her only story. Pitying your parent sucks. Anyway, I couldn't really talk to my mother about my complicated feelings about Isaiah Moss. I talked about them with Dr. Midge, of course, but she just listened in German.

"You're a teacher." It wasn't really a question, and it wasn't really a statement, just a few words hanging out together. "Nice to have summers off when you've got a sweet cabin."

"What do you do?" I asked, in lieu of a response. She studied me with those yellow-brown eyes for a moment, as if deciding how to answer.

"I cash checks from a grateful nation," she said. "And I drink."

There was a pause then, as we sat in semi-proximate silence, holding empty beer bottles and looking out at the water.

"You haven't asked about my legs." May opened a fourth bottle. She'd worked through the Heinekens, so this was a Stella. She either didn't notice or didn't care. "I think this is the longest conversation I've had with a guy who hasn't asked about my legs. Women are usually too polite." I looked down at her truncated limbs and then back up at her face.

"What legs?"

We both laughed then, long and hard. I don't know what made me say it. I'm not usually funny or bold in conversation with beautiful women. That was my father's gift. But I'd been sleeping in his bed and using his Remington and drinking his Beam, and who knows, maybe there was some of him in me after all.

The next thing I knew, May twisted with an explosive suddenness, rotating on her hip and thrusting out with her arms. Her open palms made blunt contact with my side, shoving me with violent and skilled force entirely off the pier and into the water. While the morning promised a hot July day, Franklin Lake wouldn't warm up much before August, so the unexpected dunking took my breath away. It was only three or four feet deep this close to the shore, and I was soon able to get my feet under me, finding purchase in the slimy mix of leaves and pine needles coating the lake bed under the shade of Ruby Pierce's trees. As I stood, gasping and sopping in my drenched clothes, my head was a little lower than May's. She was sitting upright on the edge of pier staring at me, and there was a frigid fury in her eyes that made Franklin Lake feel like a hot tub.

"You don't get to joke about my legs. Understand?"

Before I could even begin to frame a response, she scuttled across the dock on her hands and hoisted herself onto a low bench. She pulled a kind of compression sock over her residual limbs and then with practiced fluidity, and even a certain feral grace, inserted them into the sockets of sleek prosthetic legs. Without a backward glance she stalked stiffly back into the Pierce cottage.

It was like coming up from a basement shelter and seeing that a tornado had obliterated your house and all the others on the street. There hadn't been a cloud in the sky, no warning, and then suddenly a force of nature came out of nowhere with terrible destructive force. *No,* I thought, *not out of nowhere.* I thought I'd been so damn clever. What I'd been was a jerk. Well, not entirely. I didn't have a ton of experience with amputees, but Arcadia School was just down the road from Walter Reed Army Medical Center in Bethesda and the military's foremost treatment facility for active duty personnel who had lost limbs on the battlefield. We had a couple of students over the years with parents in uniform, and one was missing an arm, left behind in Fallujah. A prosthetist came in to speak to an assembly one day, and she told us that people generally have three reactions to meeting an amputee. One group stares, is uncomfortable, and fixates on the missing limb, while another asks an endless series of well-intentioned but invasive questions. The third group, the one we were encouraged to try to inhabit, treated the amputee like anyone else.

I'd been shooting for group three and missed the mark by a wide margin. Still standing up to my navel in Franklin

Lake, I stared at the cottage door where May had disappeared. If I wanted to see her again, I had some fences to mend. And I didn't have a great track record as a fence-mender.

~~~

I had a girlfriend back in Maryland. At least, there was a girl, and we'd been sleeping together for a couple of months, for what that was worth. I think it meant more to her than it did to me, and I think in her mind she was my girlfriend. Her name was Juliet, and maybe a lifetime with that name had saddled her with unrealistic notions of romance. I'm not saying she thought I was her true love, but I was fairly certain she believed in such a thing, and it would have been convenient for her if it was me. I wasn't in love with Juliet. I liked her, enough to sleep with her, but I was a failed writer and probably clinically depressed, so it didn't take much. It was probably the depression that drew her to me in the first place, that ambiguous sense of flawed mystery that attracts certain women to certain men. Frankly, it surprised me that Juliet was one of them. After all, she was a biology teacher, and should have known better. A fellow literature teacher, sure, or maybe French I could understand, but science? Then again, she was only twenty-four and just out of graduate school. She didn't really know anything yet. Of course, I was forty-three and I didn't know anything yet either.

I remember lying in bed in her little apartment one Sunday morning the weekend before my father died, just after we had sex to put off grading homework. If we were in a movie, we would have shared a cigarette, but in real life I've never known anyone to smoke after sex. A few before, especially in college, but none after. My usual experiences with post-coital bliss were either falling asleep or hurriedly dressing to beat traffic. But Juliet, bless her heart, she liked to talk afterwards.

"Where did you grow up?" she asked that Sunday morning, both of us wrapped in a quilt her grandmother had made. The patches of material had little kittens on it doing different household tasks, like washing dishes or planting flowers, and the images were realistically drawn in a way that made me uncomfortable. I never much liked animals doing human things. Why did some of them wear clothes and some didn't? Why did some wear a shirt and no pants? According to my mother, Mickey Mouse always made me cry as a little boy. I still wasn't partial to the arrogant little rat.

It was one of those gray drizzly mornings you can get from Maryland in May, but there was enough dusky light seeping into the room that I could see her eyes, the tangle of her hair, the tops of her breasts. Juliet was young, so she had excellent breasts, round and unapologetic. Her nose was pert and upturned, her cheeks full and rosy. She was pretty, she was young, she was useless. *Well, not* entirely *useless.* To avoid answering her, I reached out and stroked her left nipple, brushing it lightly with the tip of my right ring finger. She smiled, showing the kind of straight teeth only the daughter of a Potomac orthodontist can have. I knew all about her, the harvest of weeks of listening to her running post-orgasmic narrative. I had gotten away with it, not paying strict attention while perfectly content not to choose between reliving my own past or concocting lies I'd have to remember. Apparently twenty-four years of suburban white girlhood only takes so long to tell, and now it was my turn.

"Oscar," she said, pulling that stupid quilt up to her neck, a firm signal that recess was over and it was time to sing for my supper. "Where did you grow up?" I suppressed a sigh. I didn't begrudge her the question, or the interest, which I found mildly flattering. I was just weary to death of myself. I wondered how Isaiah Moss managed his bed-hopping all those years, answering question after question from his various conquests. Maybe the women he slept with were less inquisitive. I thought of my mother, something I usually tried not to do when I was naked in bed with an attractive woman. After they finished, I bet she told him it was nice, honey. *Never the same thing twice.* Yes, my father knew what he was doing.

"Who says I did?" It occurred to me that people might just smoke after sex for something to do with their mouths other than talk. A weak shaft of sunlight leaked through the clouds and lit up the room with a dull golden glow. Lazy motes of dust hung in the air, not really falling or floating or doing anything at all. They just sat there in their midair indolence, content to be without direction or intention. I envied that contentment.

Juliet, you sweet, innocent creature. And what did that make me? A monster, a child of a troglodyte. I had no desire for emotional intimacy in that moment, no yearning for a magical connection with another soul in this lonely trudge of life. I didn't really care about Juliet all that much beyond the ten nude minutes she gave me two or three times a week when I could shut it all out and be sweaty and selfish and absent. Fifteen minutes if I could manage it. That disconnect, that casual self-gratification, made me feel like my father, and that electricity was more potent than any orgasm.

She was still staring at me from her burrito of industrious kittens, a thick strand of her honey-blonde hair errant and loose in front of her face. It shone with an almost metallic luster in the dim light, and I thought of the twenty-odd bottles of shampoos and creams and conditioners and lotions that crowded her snug bathroom, the ones I'd scan the labels on while killing time in the shower.

"Fuller body, more bounce," I murmured, giving her wayward lock a playful little tug. She tucked it behind her ear and her eyebrows crinkled together in a brief expression of hurt, as though I'd caught her in a lie. *And wasn't it?* It's all lies, the things we do to our bodies with razors and tweezers and underwear that conceals or reveals, sucks in or props up. Has there ever been a bigger con job than the WonderBra? It's all lies we tell ourselves, that we tell the world. Our real selves aren't glossy or slick. At least, mine wasn't. I felt absurdly guilty. It was as though I had teased a toddler by hiding her toy, or maybe walked with muddy shoes on a floor one of those stupid quilt-kittens had freshly swept.

"New York. Connecticut. Mom was restless. But mostly Connecticut."

"Did she move around for work?"

"Sure."

"What did she do?"

"Mom was an actress." It was an easier answer than listing all the low-wage, dead-end jobs mom held after she gave up on acting. After she had me.

"Oh?" Juliet perked up. This was why I never talked about my father. All of a sudden, it wasn't about me anymore. "Have I seen her in anything?"

We were flirting with more truth than I really wanted to disclose. I didn't like lying, but telling the truth wasn't my favorite either. I was beginning to lose patience with the interview and wanted to either go back to sleep or grade some papers. Other than sex, taking a red pen to fractured high school prose was one of the few pleasures in my life. You haven't lived until you've seen a sixteen year old linebacker try to *spell* linebacker.

"I don't know," I replied, colder than I had intended. "Do you watch much 70s porn?"

I rolled into a sitting position, liberating myself from the kittens and the discomfort. In truth, my mother had never done any truly dirty movies that I knew about, though she'd certainly appeared in a few low-budget projects that came damn close. Even Justice Potter Stewart with his famous declaration of knowing pornography when he saw it would have struggled with categorizing some of her filmography.

"Oscar…" Juliet's fingers grazed my bare back as I sat on the bed, facing away from her. There was hurt in her voice, but hope too, and I didn't know which I regretted giving her more.

"Forget it," I said. I didn't have the energy or the courage for explanations or emotions just then. *When did I ever?* "I'm sorry." It was the last thing I said to her before I pulled on my pants and left.

I hadn't seen Juliet since. I ignored her messages on my phone when my father died, when I drove north with his ashcan, when I found his manuscript. The texts and voice mails piled up like newspapers at a vacationing homeowner's front step. The prospect of wading through them, of listening to her concern or seeing her little hug emojis, exhausted me. I knew that the longer I waited the worse it would get. I also knew that I was being an asshole, and that exhausted me too. "It's easy to make people go away," Isaiah Moss had written in one of his books, I couldn't remember which one. "It's making them stay that's hard."

I pictured Juliet, young, pretty, pissed off. Her soft golden hair back in that sloppy ponytail, her soft brown eyes sad and confused behind those round glasses she liked to wear. Her features kept eliding, diffusing, and it was May's face that stared back at me.

It took one and a half rings before Juliet answered.

"Are you all right?" she asked. Her tone was clipped and wary, but I could sense the suppressed tsunami of other stuff behind it, of concern and anger and hurt.

"More or less," I replied. "I'm sorry I haven't called, Juliet. It's been a weird time."

"I can understand that." Like so many of us, Juliet had more than one face. There was the romantic cat-quilt fawn, and the clinical falcon. When the falcon emerged from its hood, when her ruthless scientist's brain took control, there was an almost predatory detachment to Juliet. I kind of liked the falcon more than the fawn. You can respect a falcon. A falcon knows how to look out for itself. The falcon was on the phone now, and I could tell it was studying its prey. "I just want to help."

"You can't." My voice was flat, emotionless. I was glad it was the falcon. That would make this easier. "I don't think anyone can." There was a long pause. I could hear her breathing, and I thought briefly about Sunday mornings in her bed. It had been nice. Cloying, claustrophobic, unsustainable, but nice. It can be hard to let nice things go, even when you've always known they aren't really yours.

"You don't have to worry about me, Oscar." Her voice had gone cool, hard, shielded. The fawn forever fled. "Worry about yourself. That's all you really care about anyway." And the line went dead. I sighed. Faculty meetings at Arcadia would be frostier next year.

~~~

May was back in the water the next morning. Diamonds glittered in her wake as she knifed her graceful line through the cove, turning with surgical precision every fifty meters to retrace her route. I loaded up the metal bucket with beers from the cellar and threaded that narrow dirt path through the blueberries and Queen Anne's lace and black-eyed Susans growing wild along the shoreline. At the Pierce pier, I sat on the bench next to May's carbon fiber legs. She kept swimming, each arm breaking the surface in turn and thrusting forward to grab the next stretch of lake with her relentless stroke. It was hypnotic, a tiger pacing in its cage at the zoo or the pendulum of a great clock marking the long arc of its time. I reached into the bucket and took one of the cold bottles. It was sweating already in the morning heat, the back of my neck and my armpits responding with their own damp prickle. I rubbed the green glass with my thumb, feeling the cool smooth wetness of it, then I uncapped it with a bottle opener. I had none of the savage skill necessary for May's method. I sipped for a while in silence, watching her swim. A light breeze, warm and westerly, ruffled the leaves of the birches without ever touching the water, but all else was still.

After some minutes had passed, she carved slowly back to the pier, languid and unhurried. She climbed the ladder with her arms, unsurprised to see me when she turned to collect her towel. This one was green, with blue sharks smiling secret cotton smiles. She nodded at the bucket as she rubbed her bristly yellow hair with the sharks.

"Now you're getting the hang of it," May said. I brought over a Heineken, and she took it.

"About yesterday," I began, and she waved her free hand in the air, prying the beer open against the edge of the dock with the other.

"Water under the bridge. Or is it over the dam?" She took a long drink. "You're the English teacher. Which one is it?"

"I don't teach English," I replied. "I teach Literature."

"There's a difference?"

"An English teacher would say that both idioms mean the same thing. That water has passed by and there's nothing we can do about it. We can't change the past."

"A literature teacher wouldn't say that?"

"We would, but we would take it past language and into symbolism. Dams are designed to stop water, whereas bridges are designed to allow it to pass. When water has gone under the bridge, things are working properly. When water has gone over the dam, things have gone wrong. There's been some failure. There's an element of regret to water passing over the dam."

"I see." May looked away, staring off into the low, streaky white clouds for a moment. Then she raised her bottle toward me. "Water over the dam, then."

I brought my bottle into contact with hers with a faint clink.

"Fair enough. I am sorry, May. I didn't mean to be a jerk."

"Jerks rarely do," she replied, with her habitual toss of her empty bottle into the middle of the cove. "Well, except maybe your pop. He seemed to relish it."

"Yeah, it was a bit of a personality trait."

"I tried to read his books, you know," May said, shrugging. She had a great shrug, the byproduct of great shoulders. It made her entire body move in a way that left me dry in the mouth. "Never finished any of them. I couldn't see what the big deal was. I'm also not a huge fan of raging assholes."

She wasn't the first person ever to dislike my father's work, of course, but I felt an absurd surge of gratitude for it. Isaiah Moss was one of those writers that you were just supposed to say you liked because it made you sound smart. People claimed to have read his books even when they hadn't, like with Tolstoy, or Joyce, or the Bible. As far as being an asshole went, my father exhibited genuine bewilderment when people dismissed his writing because they didn't like him or his reputation. "They say I'm not kind enough," he said once in a Vanity Fair interview. "I find it unrealistic to expect someone to be the most gifted person in any room and also the nicest." He went on to imply that the one might preclude the other. "Brilliance can be paralyzing. To know yourself capable of producing timeless art but to realize that most of what you create is mortal horseshit is depressing. And you want me to be pleasant?"

On the other side of the cottage from my father's cabin was another dwelling, a little less shopworn and sheepish than either the Pierce or Moss establishments. It seemed to have been painted more recently than the Reagan administration, a midnight blue with bright white three-inch trim around new windows. The second story opened onto a sprawling porch made from the kind of artificial materials preferred by city folk disinterested in re-staining every few years. Somebody was in residence, for the week or the summer, because children were splashing in the shallows where a little beach had been installed, illegally-dumped sand cupping the lake with intimate firmness like a lover's hand on a breast. A dowdy middle-aged woman in a skirted floral one-piece sat in a low chair at the lake's edge under a floppy hat, her face buried in some cheap paperback, Patterson or Koontz or something equally vapid. May seemed vaguely irritated by the frolicking, her thin eyebrows knitting together, a marriage of anorexic caterpillars.

We sat for a little while, not talking, just drinking beer, letting July have its way with us. Sometimes, if you just shut the fuck up for a minute and be in a time and place without regard for before or after, the world can be a pretty decent place. There was so much green and blue in the sky and the trees and the water, hues no paint store could hope to duplicate, no matter how pretentious the name of the shade.

Summer Day Blue, Hopeless Periwinkle, Forest Orgasm. May's eyes were closed, her head tilted back, the sun and beer and quiet softening the jagged edges of her cheek, of her jaw, of her collarbone. She had on the same suit as the day before, and it hugged her so closely that her every line was apparent, an inky sketch against the pastel palate of the cove. My eyes drank her in, the Heineken warming forgotten in my hand. She was carved from erotic marble, the Venus de Milo with arms instead of legs. There was something untamed about her, a wildness, the terrifying and exciting prospect that she might say or do just about anything. Her thighs were as muscled as the rest of her, thin and yet far from gaunt, crisscrossed with puckered white scarring. They both ended just below her quadriceps, above where her knees should have been, round stumps with a thin pink line running from side to side.

"Having a good look?" she asked. Her eyes were still closed, but somehow she knew I was looking. People were probably always looking.

"I'm sorry," I said again.

"Don't apologize any more. I'm trying to like you and it's getting in the way."

Whatever game the children had been playing evolved from chirps of juvenile joy into shrieks, the kind of pleasure-screams children emit that can be hard to differentiate between glee and peril, and they had crept closer to the Pierce dock. I suspected they wanted to ask if they could use it for running and jumping into the water but were hesitant, either because of May's unusual appearance or their own lack of courage. There was a boy, brown haired with an eight-year old's chubbiness sagging over his aquamarine suit, and two girls. They were younger, maybe five or six in their pigtails and strapped-on floaties, and they were doing the bulk of the screeching. A corner of May's mouth twitched, her mounting displeasure evident.

She did a sort of half-barrel roll then, nimble and preposterous, and began putting her legs on. Once she was on her artificial feet, she draped the towel over her shoulders and cocked her head to one side, focused on me rather than the dissonance next door.

"When's the last time you had an actual meal?" she asked. "Or has it been a steady diet of Campbell's and microwave popcorn over there?"

It was a little unnerving to look up at her like that, a supplicant at the foot of some golden goddess, graven against the sapphire firmament above. The sun was directly behind her, illuminating her with a fiery corona I had to squint against. I raised one hand to shield my eyes and tried to remember the last time I hadn't eaten out of a can.

"Hey," I said, "I've got one of those big plastic tubs of cheese balls over there. I'm happy to share."

"No thanks. I prefer my empty calories in liquid form. Tell you what, come to dinner tonight. Gram and I will put some real food in you for a change."

One of the little girls had ventured too close, and her vigorous splashing reached May's back. Not a lot, not a soaking, just a little bit of water, but May jerked away from it like acid and spun to face the offender so quickly that her prosthetic foot caught in the boards of the dock and she nearly fell.

"Get away from me!" she shouted, both of her hands curving into white-fingered fists. She was visibly vibrating with rage, pale and taut and shaking. "Get the fuck out of here! Right now!" She continued to unleash a leather-lunged tirade of vulgarity for a full minute while the girl floated in stunned paralysis. I was just as mute and motionless, as was the woman in her chair. May's overreaction to the mildest kind of horseplay was so abrupt and brutal that we were both caught completely off guard. Then, as suddenly as it began, it was over, a violent cloudburst that had spent its charge. May didn't apologize, didn't even look at either of us, before placing both of her hands over her face and stumbling back toward the cottage, a tin nymph on tin legs, half-carved by Aphrodite, half-sculpted by Hephaestus and well on her way to Hades.

Moss

CHAPTER FOUR

It was one of those evenings you get in New England summers, when the heat of the day reluctantly fades and the sun lingers just at the horizon. Gloaming, the Scots poets had called it, the dusky bridge from day to night, a rosy pre-twilight where trees and rocks and our own flesh assume a gauzy unreality. "Gie me the hour o' 64loamin' grey," wrote Robbie Burns, "it maks my heart sae cheery O." I stood for a minute or two on the shoulder of the dirt road, staring past darkening trunks to the still waters of Franklin Lake. A bullfrog from the creek gave a lusty, baritone thrum, secure in his damp masculinity. I wondered how many times my father had looked up from his typewriter at this tranquility, this gentle end of day. There was enough poetry in his prose that he must have paused in his labors from time to time to breathe in the beauty of it.

There was a homey squatness to the Pierce cabin next door. It was a simple brown log structure nestled in a wooded dell behind a split-rail fence, a well-tended flower garden embracing either side of the paving stone walkway. I didn't know their names, but there were tall pink blossoms and short red ones, with splashes of yellow and orange all fading into gray-green as the light ebbed. Windows flanked the front door, and a warm glow spilled through them into the waning day. A large, unruly lilac stood sentinel to one side, no longer in season, its blooms faded from whatever white or purple spring had given them. I found Ruby there, puttering amongst her plants, amidst the gathering gloom and assembling mosquitoes, a beardless garden gnome brought to life.

"Isaiah's boy," she said, peering up at me beadily.

"So my mom says." I wasn't sure how she would react to me, given how dismissive I'd been at our first meeting a few days earlier.

"Your mother. The *actress*." The word was a dismissive curse, her voice the crumpling of stiff paper, glottal and harsh. She made a noise with her mouth I'd never heard before, the bastard child of a cluck and chuckle. It occurred to me then, for the first time, that this woman might well have regarded my mother as a rival for the affections of my father. The idea was ludicrous. *Wasn't it?*

"Your flowers are lovely," I said, both to change the subject and because that's what I'd heard people say about their neighbors' flower gardens on television. She nodded a wordless New Hampshire thank you.

"There was a dog from the Eaton place up the road," Ruby said, her small hand in its floral-print gardening glove waving vaguely in that direction. She straightened up, but even erect her body was still gnomish. "Eaton, that insurance thief from down Portsmouth way." I couldn't tell if she meant that Eaton was the beneficiary of insurance fraud, or that he sold overpriced insurance. I didn't ask.

"It was a spaniel, a shaggy black and white one. And he was a stealthy little mutt. He'd sneak around and crap all over my flowerbeds." The way she said "crap" was percussive, a verbal thunderclap, the terminal P bitten in half like a fresh carrot. "One day, this spring, I was out here pulling weeds, and I see him up there by the mailbox. I told him to git, but he just sat there looking at me, thinking about crapping. So I picked up a rock, a decent one, about the size of a baseball. I made like I was going to throw it at him to scare him off, but he just kept right on sitting and looking and thinking about crapping." Ruby paused to scratch her flat nose, leaving a smudge of black earth across her face. She swatted at a mosquito and carried on. "I threw the rock, and I killed that dog dead on the spot. Laid his skull open like an overripe peach."

Jesus.

"Anyway, I couldn't take him down to Eaton. That fella strikes me as the suing sort. So instead I cut him into a few pieces and buried him here and there." She pointed around the flower garden. "Damndest thing. Best fertilizer I've ever had."

We studied each other for a long moment.

"Mrs. Pierce, that dog wasn't the only one full of shit."

She laughed, an honest and raucous sound accompanied by a wooden, hacking smoker's cough.

"Maybe."

We stood there for a moment, ringed by flowers and shadows.

"Mrs. Pierce," I began.

"Ruby, boy."

"Ruby. I wanted to ask about this morning on the dock."

"Mind your business." She stepped closer to me, tiny and suddenly solemn. "Don't pry. And don't bother May with that nonsense, you hear?"

"Yes ma'am."

"Good. Now, are you," she pointed slowly at me, then to the interior of the cottage, "coming inside?"

Busted. I tilted my head, shrugged, and half-bowed an apology. "After you, ma'am."

"Keep your ma'am, I don't want it. Well, my grand-daughter made me promise to feed you, so we'd better head on in before these skeeters drain us dry."

I wasn't sure what to expect inside the Pierce cabin. My only experience with these little midcentury lakefront places was my dad's place next door, and that was a fairly unre-markable, utilitarian space. Admittedly, the view was spec-tacular. My father's cabin, my cabin now, had no sense of place, little decoration, almost no evidence of the man who had spent years there writing. *Other than the typewriter and the case of Jim Beam in the closet, of course.* Here it was smaller, much cozier, much more inhabited. The walls were pine paneling, the floor carpeted in tight burgundy Berber. There was a galley kitchen, avocado-green 70s-era appliances and bright lemon 60s-era linoleum flooring, with a well-loved trestle dining table and benches nearby. Plants were every-where – cut flowers on end tables, ferns on windowsills, a surly cactus on the Formica kitchen counter. This was a space alive, a comfortable and comforting contrast to the arid sterility of the Scrotum.

And there were books.

Man, there were books.

The already snug living room was cramped even more by a wall-length floor-to-ceiling bookcase overflowing with books. Stacks of books rose from the floor like stalagmites, elbowed their way alongside lamps, and curled on the couch like ill-behaved dogs. These were real books, too, not just the airport paperback thrillers or Reader's Digest condensed versions on hand for summer reading at less erudite seasonal cabins. Scanning the spines I saw Faulkner and Hardy, Cervantes and Shakespeare, Austen and Dostoyevsky among the hundreds of classics crowding the haphazard shelves.

"Gram's a reader."

May was curled up on the couch in a fuzzy plum-colored sweater with a high floppy neck that came up to her chin and a lap blanket over her legs, cupping a glass of red wine with one hand and stroking a gray shorthaired cat with the other. It was the first time I'd seen her in clothes. It softened her somehow, bringing rondure to her sharp edges.

"So I see," I said. "Hi."

"Hi." She glanced at the cat. "This is Ophelia," she said by way of introduction. The cat ignored me with casual feline indifference.

"There's rosemary," I said idly. "That's for remembrance." May looked at me quizzically. Before I could explain, Ruby came in from washing off the gardening, rubbing her hands with a kitchen towel.

"And there is pansies, that's for thoughts." One of my eyebrows rose in surprise. I looked at the old woman appraisingly. *Huh. Let's see what she's got.*

"There's fennel for you, and columbines," I continued. "There's rue for you, and here's some for me. We may call it herb of grace o'Sundays."

"O, you must wear your rue with a difference!" The old woman didn't miss a beat. She mimicked handing me a flower. "There's a daisy." Her glasses had slid down her nose, and she looked at me expectantly over the tortoiseshell frames.

"I would give you some violets," I replied, and I was surprised by a sudden catch in my throat as I completed the line. "But they wither'd all when my father died."

"Have you two gone nuts?" May asked from the couch, her thin lips curved into a bemused smirk.

"That's the essence of the thing," Ruby said. "Time to tend to dinner." And she shuffled back into the kitchen area.

"Ophelia," I told May. "When she's losing her mind in the fourth act of Hamlet, she describes the flowers in her bouquet. Literature, remember? I'm surprised your grandmother knows it so well."

"Gram's a reader," May repeated, taking a swallow of wine.

"Bullshit," I said. "Your grandmother is more than that."

"Table needs setting!" Ruby barked as she took a large roast bird out of the oven and set it on the counter before turning to fiddle with two or three stainless steel pots on the range.

"I'm happy to help," I said, "though I don't know where anything is."

"I'm on it," May replied.

"Oh, don't get up," I protested, but she had swung herself into a lightweight wheelchair and rolled the dining area where she gathered cutlery and white dinner plates from a battered wooden hutch, pivoting to arrange them on the table.

"You can fetch a bottle of Beaujolais from downcellar," Ruby pointed at a door. "Better fetch two," she amended. The door stuck just a little but came open with a resigned pop after a couple of tugs. A long string dangled from the ceiling, and when I pulled it a single light bulb came on, illuminating simple wooden plank stairs descending into a dungeon of rock and earth. On the way down I noticed iron handles bolted into the handrail and along the unmortared walls. I tried to picture May swinging her way down here and back up, but clearly she did it enough that the accommodations had been installed. Not for the first time, I wondered about who she was. More accurately, who she had been. Where Juliet had been a developing Polaroid you had to hold carefully by the edges, May was a battered snapshot, with smudged thumbprints and a tear in one corner. Clearly her disability wasn't something she'd been born with – the scarring on her legs testified to that, as well as her line the day before about collecting checks from the government. May Pierce intrigued me, and I hadn't been intrigued in a very long time. The curiosity was seductive. I wondered if that was how Juliet had felt about me, if that explained all her questions. If it had been, maybe I'd been a bastard to keep her at arm's length. *No,* I told myself, *she's better off. You'd have been a bastard to let her in.*

What books were to the living room, wines were to the basement. A decrepit washing machine and dryer sat stacked atop each other at the foot of the stairs, the Adam and Eve of all the Maytags ever made, but the rest of the low chamber was given over to pine racks drilled into the living rock, laden to groaning. There had to be at least three hundred bottles down there. *Booze,* I thought, *and books and sex. Maybe Ruby Pierce had been my father's soulmate.* It took a while to locate the Beaujolais among the bottles. As with the bookshelves upstairs, there appeared to be no order or rhyme to their placement. It was a lawless riot of red and white down there, an anarchic utopia of wine. I eventually managed to find what I'd been sent after and made my way back up the rickety steps to rejoin the Pierce ladies.

In the hallway I noticed a picture on the wall, a young man in drab Army greens and camouflage helmet, leaning on his rifle. He was skinny but handsome, with a cleft chin that made him resemble a kind of underfed Cary Grant. His face was sweat-streaked and he looked tired, but he was smiling against the lush green backdrop of jungle. In neat black cursive script was written "For My Ruby".

"Mister Pierce?" I asked.

"That is Private First Class Langdon Pierce," Ruby said, joining me at the picture. She barely came up to my shoulder as she stood next to me. "Langdon had been an Eagle Scout, you see, and in those days that would get you a first class rating. Most enlisted men would have to wait a year for that step." She reached out and straightened the frame, though it hadn't looked crooked to me. Her fingers lingered on the glass, almost a caress. "He was a Bethlehem Pierce, mind you, not one of those Concord Pierces like drunk old Franklin." She said Bethlehem in two frigid syllables, *Beth-lem*, with that charmless rustic habit New Englanders had of naming their towns after world cities and then changing the pronunciation so it wouldn't seem pretentious.

"We graduated from high school together in the spring of 1965," she continued. "Before June was out, we were married and Lang was at Fort Dix for basic. He wasn't drafted, he chose to go. Boys were still choosing to go then. By September he was shipped off and I was left pregnant with May's mother."

"Don't bore Oscar, Gram," May called, back on the couch, under the blanket, content with wine and cat.

"Oh, I'm not bored." I wasn't being polite. I had a fascination with family history, probably because I didn't really have one of my own. My mother had lost touch with her parents when she fled home for a glamorous life in acting, and I had no clue who my father's were. As far as I knew, Isaiah Moss had spontaneously appeared like the elder gods, fully-grown, clutching a bottle of bourbon in one hand and a typewriter ribbon in the other. Ruby relieved me of both bottles of wine. Displaying a surgeon's skill with a manual corkscrew, she had one open and breathing in seconds.

"Chicken's done resting," she said, and set to carving it.

May was right, I realized. It had been too long since I'd enjoyed a real dinner. I subsisted on a steady diet of take-out in Maryland, relying on pickup hoops with the varsity boys at Arcadia a couple of times a week to slow the advance of my middle-aged paunch. And while I wasn't exactly going hungry at my father's cabin, Campbell's and Jim Beam can only do so much. The chicken came to the table alongside gravy, stuffing, mashed potatoes, green beans, and fresh-baked rolls. The mouth-watering aroma made me think of my mom. She didn't read much, and she was a lousy actress, but the woman could cook.

"Thank you," I said as I sat, and little more was said over the next several minutes as the three of us tucked in with enthusiasm. Benjamin Franklin once wrote to a friend, perhaps joking, perhaps not, suggesting that extramarital affairs were better with older women. "When women cease to be handsome," the ribald old satyr had written, "they study to be good...they supply the Diminution of Beauty by an Augmentation of Utility. There is hardly such a thing to be found as an old woman who is not a good woman." I began to see his point. Of course, Franklin also noted that older paramours were less likely to get pregnant and were "so grateful". While my father had followed the entirety of Big Ben's bawdy counsel, Ruby Pierce's simple, delectable cooking was enough for me. Eventually sated, we sat and drank wine while digesting. Ruby was a devotee of the grape, and two bottles of Beaujolais became four.

"If you never empty your glass, and simply keep filling it, you've just had the one." She winked at me, an unsettling convulsion of one of her gimlet eyes. The more wine Ruby put away, the more voluble she became, talking at length about flowers and books – though never Isaiah Moss – and eventually she found her way back to the subject of May's grandfather.

"Lang had just turned nineteen," Ruby said. Other than loosening her sharp tongue and enhancing her Yankee accent, the wine did little to slow her down. She gripped her long-stemmed glass with one sclerotic claw, staring down the dirty dishes on the table as though they'd wash themselves if she glared at them hard enough. "It was November of '65 and his company was in the Ia Drang Valley."

"Vietnam," May said, her voice uncharacteristically soft. "Grandpa was 7th Cav." The night was deepening into a violet velvet out the window, quiet but for the stray desultory hoot of a forlorn owl. "Bravo Company."

"He had just turned nineteen," Ruby repeated. "He didn't know that in a few months his daughter would be born. He didn't know that in a few days he'd be dead." She looked out the window, where full dark had descended over the lake. Loons called to each other, fireflies glowed in their random dance, and an old woman retreated more than fifty years into the past.

We drank our wine to occupy our hands and our mouths. The silence was so oppressive that I wanted to say something, just to make it stop, but the look on May's face told me to shut the fuck up for a change. For a change, I did.

"Most of what I know, I found out later," Ruby said. "Letters from other men in Lang's unit, books written about the war. Lang and the 7th Cav, they were pinned down at some place called LZ Albany near the Cambodian border."

"LZ means landing zone. It's a clearing where helicopters can land to drop off or pick up troops." May had a different kind of faraway look in her eyes, and I knew her mind was conjuring a more vivid, more professionally drawn image of the battlefield than was her grandmother's. *She's seen an LZ or two of her own,* I surmised, *and maybe left her legs at one.* Ruby continued as if no one had spoken.

"They were crossing that clearing when the Viet Cong hit them hard. Bravo Company lost half their men in five minutes of fire. Dozens of boys, bleeding their last in that idiotic jungle. And no one's been able to tell me why, not for fifty years. The best anyone can ever manage is 'God and Country'. Not enough. Not near enough, not for me." She gulped from her glass and her hand trembled, slopping some of the wine over the rim. She was finally getting drunk. I was surprised it had taken this long and this much. "Moore now, that damned high-horse Colonel, the one with all the medals from Korea, he knew it was 10-1 against him but he thought he was bulletproof. He thought each American boy was worth ten pajama monkeys and that evened the odds. Fool. Hell, 7th Cav was Custer's regiment. Hubris. Him. Us. Our precious American Empire. Same dumb-assed story over and over. And our kids keep paying the freight.

"The postman came to the farm with that damned telegram. 'The Secretary of the Army has asked me to express his deep regrets…' I took that Western Union telegram and I fell to my knees, pregnant out to here and I screamed and cursed the Army and Colonel Moore and Lyndon Johnson and America herself. I screamed and I hated this country and I hated my husband. I hated every soul who ever drew breath. I hated so hard that I went into labor. The next day, May 15, '66, our daughter was born." She looked at May almost in surprise, as though she'd forgotten she was there. "Your mother."

Ruby was gazing out the window again, though there was nothing there to see.

"'When lilacs last in the dooryard bloom'd, and the great star early droop'd in the western sky at night…'"

"'I mourned, and yet shall mourn with ever-returning spring.'" I finished the verse quietly, and May shook her head.

"I know my Whitman as well as you know your Army acronyms," I told her.

"Whitman was a racist and a prick." Ruby bit off the words like meat from a strip of jerky. The sorrowful, soulful young widow was gone, and the crotchety old woman my father used to screw was back. "But he could write the hell out of a poem."

"Lilacs," I said, thinking of the Pierce cabin dooryard I'd seen earlier that evening.

"Gone by," Ruby slurred, her old eyes red and watery and tired. "Lilacs flower in May."

"I saw yours," I replied gently. "Even gone by. And my father's next door."

"Same plant, his a cutting from mine," she whispered. "Kindred spirits."

"'April is the cruelest month, breeding lilacs out of the dead land,'" I said. It was the opening line of T.S. Eliot's *The Waste Land*, a poem I'd assigned to my students like every other literature teacher. Ruby didn't look at me as she recited from a later section, instead reading the words as they scrolled across her impressive memory.

"'He who was living is now dead. We who were living are now dying with a little patience.'" It was abundantly evident that she had read all of those books jumbled in the cottage, probably more than once. Ruby did look at me then, a sad woman who had been sad for a long time. "You know, Eliot was a schoolteacher, too."

~~~

After we washed the dishes, May escorted me out onto the dock behind her grandmother's cabin on her wobbly artificial legs. We might as well have been on the surface of some wet alien planet, the only souls in the universe. There was a satin quality to the lake at night. Water and shore and sky met in the same rich indigo drapery, the unclouded stars a million million gaudy sequins sewn into Nox's sable mantle. It was quiet even more than it was dark, and I could feel May next to me more than I could see her, though the starlight gave her sharp features a pastel softness, vague and pale. *She walks in beauty, like the night, of cloudless climes and starry skies, and all that's best of dark and bright meet in her aspect and her eyes*...except May wasn't the kind of porcelain drawing-room beauty Byron was writing about. The final stanza felt even more wrong: *A mind at peace with all below, a heart whose love is innocent*. Peace and innocence were not words that came to mind when contemplating May Pierce.

"When I was small," I said in lieu of more poetry, my voice too loud even as I whispered, "my mother would sing me to sleep at night. She has a nice voice, you know? A mom's singing is always good anyway, I think, but mine could actually carry a tune. I guess she did some musical theater when she was young, before she tried to make it as an actress, before she met my father." We stood there, in the silent dark. I think both of us wanted the evening to last just a little longer. I think both of us were in that wonderful drunken middle ground, that Goldilocks sweet spot where inhibitions wither yet faculties remain. "Anyway, she would sing about all the animals going to sleep. All the dogs, all the cats, all the rabbits, and so on. 'All the squirrels are asleep... all the foxes are asleep...' that sort of thing. I would try to stay awake to hear about all the different animals, and she'd just keep coming up with them. Sometimes I could last long enough that she'd start in on Africa, on lions and hippos and stuff." I paused, listening, but all was quiet. "All the birdies are asleep," I half-sang. *I should call my mom tomorrow,* I thought.

"I never knew my mother," May said softly. "So, you know, I honestly don't give a fuck about your maudlin little story."

I tried to say something, anything, but nothing would emerge past the huge lump that had suddenly lodged in my chest. I just stood there, mutely letting her rebuke hang in the air between us, a pall of unvarnished candor.

"Since we're being honest," I said, "what happened this morning? With the kids in the water?" Yeah, Ruby told me to mind my business. *This is my business,* I decided.

"The stupid Wheeler girl knows better," she said, and I couldn't see the flush on her neck and cheeks but imagined I could feel the heat rising in her radiating off her skin like a furnace. "Those kids are supposed to stay over by their shitty little beach."

"Okay..."

"Look, I don't like kids. All right? I can't have kids, so I don't like kids. Happy?"

That explains some *of that explosion earlier,* I thought, *but only some.*

"I'm sorry," she finally said, before I could manage it. "You didn't know."

"No, I'm sorry," I said, shaking my head. "Jesus, I just shook my head. I forgot that it's took dark for you to see me."

"I can see a little." I felt her hand fumble for mine, questing fingers, then she held it. Her hands were bony and strong, but not cold.

"It's funny how darkness emboldens," I said. "We think and say and do things in the dark we would never do if the lights were on."

"That explains a lot of lost virginities," May said, and I laughed. She was close, her taut body making contact with mine from shoulder to hand. I could smell her, a warm, inviting blend of red wine and woman. With the courage of darkness and drink, I leaned in to kiss her. She turned her head, and my lips found hair.

"Rein in there, cowboy." She released my hand, sliding her fingers up my forearm to the elbow, where she took a gentle but firm grip and created a little space between us. "Don't you have any women friends?"

You *took* my *hand*, I thought with a red twinge of embarrassed frustration. You *were flirting with* me. But was she? Maybe I was just reading it wrong. Maybe I read everything wrong. I tried to think about her question. I had been good friends with a woman once, so good that we got married and stopped being friends. But that had been a long time ago, and I didn't want to think about Kate at the moment, let alone talk about her. There were certainly women I was friendly with now. Colleagues at Arcadia, fellow students from grad school, the nice Korean lady in the apartment next to mine, the one with the intense Weimaraner who stared me down with velvet eyes whenever we passed in the hall. But was being friendly the same as being friends?

"I don't think I do," I said eventually. "But I can't really think of any men I'm friends with either. I don't think I'm the kind of guy who has friends."

"I'll be your friend," she said, and there was a kind of warmth to it despite the inherent rebuff. "I think you need a friend more than you need a lover."

My stomach churned for a moment, wrestling May's rejection to the ground and pinning it there, willing it to be less humiliation than it felt. I didn't want my misunderstanding to sour our connection, to sound a clumsy note against the symphonic perfection of the dark. I didn't want to be stupid, to be wrong, to be insufficient. I might as well have wished to be ten feet tall, or a world-famous writer. Sometimes you are what you are.

Change the subject, I thought with a juvenile desperation.

"May," I asked, "what happened? With your legs?"

The pause then was long and rich, a German chocolate cake of silence, fifteen Oreo cookies and a tall glass of whole milk. I began to wonder what would happen first: words spoken aloud or diabetic comas.

"We've had enough tragedy tonight," she said finally. "Go to bed, Oscar. Do you need help getting back?"

"You going to walk me home?" I asked, a little more harshly than I meant. I waved a hand by way of apology. "Nah, I'm good. I can find my way," I muttered.

"Oh Oscar," she laughed, and it was harsh but not cruel, "when have you ever found your way?"

Wordlessly, I turned and walked slowly along the dirt path back to the cabin, placing my feet carefully as I went. The last thing I needed was a half-drunk stumble on a loose pebble to put a cherry atop my mortification sundae. I knew that shaky footbridge was waiting for me, a land mine in the darkness.

"Oscar."

I couldn't really see May's face in the dark, but there was a funny sound to her voice. It sounded almost like she was near tears.

"Yeah?"

"Pick me up at seven tomorrow morning. There's some-place I want to take you."

A few minutes later I paused alone on the rickety porch behind my father's cabin, looking at the stars. My belly was full of warm, unfamiliar wine-drunk, and I still felt foolish from May's rejection. To drive out the nagging shame I thought about Ruby's stories. I thought about Langdon Pierce, about lost youth, about war and pain and death. About those left behind, who waited and worried, who lived each day and slept each night with fear instead of their loved one. I thought about my father and Korea. Isaiah Moss had never kept a war diary; at least, not one he had ever shared with the world. His third book, his most visceral and intimate, *The Meat Grinder*, delved deep into the inhumanity of warfare. Set a century before his own martial experiences, it followed members of the XXI Corps of the Union Army at the Battle of Chickamauga during the Civil War, where more than 30,000 Americans died in combat. All those Americans laid to rest, rebels and federals alike, beneath the scorched ground in companionable conflict. To Isaiah Moss, the madness of human conflict knew no calendar. Hoplites of ancient Greece, Roman legionnaires, Russian Cossacks, jack tars on Nelson's flagship, they all bled and swore and fell, anonymous wage-slaves in the foundry of empires.

Smallwood was among the first killed, but he didn't die straight off. He took his time. His body, mortally injured, struggled to live even as his mind knew he was done. After the bullets bit into his shoulder and his thigh and his gut he lay there, his eyes to the sky. That beautiful sky. The same sky he had looked up at from his father's farm in Pennsylvania as a boy, taking a break from the plowing and sowing, dreaming about growing up, about getting out, about having adventures. In his dreams, the adventures never ended with a bullet. He felt other men running past, the thunder of the hooves of the cavalry officers, the deep resonant baritone of the artillery as it belched forth the glory of the union. His arteries pulsed in slow unison, jettisoning his ichor into the churned mud, a steady symphony of slow death. The noise pounded on all sides, but his eyes, not his ears commanded his last flickering attention. It was the trees he saw, the trees he noticed. Above him they stretched, blackened and leafless, into the cold blue embrace of a cloudless sky. Trees that had stood since before Washington's inaugural, since before Jamestown's founding. Hickories and hemlocks, tall and heedless and burning. The carnage hurt his heart, and he groped for the meaning of it all. I hope it matters, *he thought as his life drained into the Tennessee dirt.* I hope we win. I hope those darkies get to go free. *He hoped, and he bled, and he died. He wasn't alone. Smallwood died at Chickamauga, with the men under Rosencrans and the trees unlucky enough to stand between the gray laundry and the blue.*

Isaiah Moss understood the futility, the waste of warfare. He'd seen it in Korea. He'd lived it in the trenches with men who never went home again. *The Meat Grinder* was in equal measure an elegy for those men and an indictment of the policies that sent them to die, an indictment of war itself. My father was never overtly political – he never went on talk shows and advocated for or against one thing or another. As much as he and Gore Vidal were drinking buddies, he was never the activist Vidal was. Isaiah Moss wrote his stories and let them speak for themselves. He found explication tedious.

I found everything tedious, myself most of all. Nothing excited me, nothing moved me. I was bereft of inspiration. And yet May Pierce intrigued me. I wrapped myself in that thin hopeful cloak and fell asleep on the sofa.

FIRST INTERLUDE

Excerpted from Wages of Empire

From the diary of Private First Class Langdon Pierce, 2nd Battalion, 7th Cavalry Regiment, recovered by the Viet Cong at Ia Drang and remitted to US military authorities after his death

July 15, 1965
We left Norfolk today on the USNS Kula Gulf. *It's a big boat. The Navy fellows insist on calling the* Kula Gulf *a ship, but no one's explained to me yet the difference between the two. Seems to me they both float the same. She's big, too. I remember thinking my grandfather's fourteen-foot sailboat at Sunapee was pretty swell. This thing is five hundred foot long if it's an inch, and crammed full with guys like me headed for the war, two thousand of us not counting the crew. They call her a baby flat-top because she used to be an aircraft carrier in WWII. She's got some planes on board headed for the war too but mostly it's men.*

I try not to think of home and the farm and Ruby (mostly Ruby) because it makes me sad that I won't see them for quite some time. I let myself dream a little bit at night, though, surrounded by the other fellows, stacked up in our bunks. It helps me to get to sleep. I'm lucky that I haven't been seasick like a lot of the boys.

Jul 21, 1965
This morning we steamed through the Panama Canal. I saw the sun rise over the Pacific and set over the Atlantic and apparently you can't see that anywhere else.

Jul 28, 1965
Refueling at Long Beach. We've been on the Kula Gulf *two weeks now and I'm getting to know the other 1st Cav guys. I guess we've got another couple of weeks across the Pacific to Vietnam. It's like a cruise but who knows if your ticket is round trip?*

Sep 18, 1965

Landed at a place called Qui Nhon. It's a pretty good-sized city, I guess. Lots of G.I.s coming in, not just us. It's hot. Sgt Coulter, our fire team leader, was in Korea and he says he never thought he'd miss it but this heat did the trick. He's a hard horse, kept us drilling even on the ride here. Told us that every bruise and blister he gives us improves our chances of getting back home. My chances should be pretty good. Now that we've landed, he says the boat was a vacation. Don't much like the sound of that. Sarge was in Korea with Col Moore, the commanding officer of 7th Cav. He says Moore was a paratrooper. Said he's the Army's best fighting officer and we're lucky to be in his regiment. Sounds good to me.

Oct 12th, 1965

Not much chance to write lately. We've been busy moving around. It's hard to remember a cool breeze or the cool swimming pond at the farm. It's been hot every day here, and wet. One of the first things Sgt Coulter taught us was to run our socks between our toes each morning before putting our boots on so we don't get foot rot. Teddy Rourke, the Irish kid from Brookline, he got bitten by a viper one night last week in his cot and lost three toes to the venom. I've slept with my boots on since then.

Nov 2, 1965

The jungle is all around. Pretty sometimes, when the sun hits the leaves a certain way, but it's hard to see it like that when there's fellows out there looking for us so they can kill us. It's hard not to see Charlie behind every tree. I never thought I'd hate the woods.

I keep thinking of that old brick church at home. Sitting in those pews on hot summer Sundays with Mom and Dad. Mom sitting upright in her pretty hat paying attention and Dad stewing because Ben and I wouldn't sit still. I don't remember much of the sermons or the readings, but I remember some of the songs. There was one. I don't remember the name, but there was a line about "when the world's sharp strife is nigh" and it asked God to protect soldiers when they take up their swords. I remember it because I asked Dad what strife meant and he told me to look it up. I've prayed more since we got here than in my whole life before. Maybe that's not how it's supposed to work but I can't go back now and pray more when I was a kid. All I can do is say my prayers now – me and all the other boys. We've got all kinds, too, Jews and Catholics and even an Arab fellow who follows Islam. Our prayers have to be along the same lines, I think. Help me make it. Or else help make it quick.

Nov 15, 1965

Tomorrow morning we're going after the landing zone, Sgt. Coulter says. It's dark tonight, no moon. Not quiet though. Lots of fellows moving around, nobody sleeping much. I don't know what to expect tomorrow. Officers say there'll be stiff resistance, but we don't really know what that means. I hope I don't have to kill anyone, at least not anyone I can see. They're just fellows over there in the pajamas, fellows doing what they're told same as us. Some of them probably have wives too, even little kids. I hope not. It'd be easier if they didn't have families. If we knew they were bad guys, not just guys on the wrong side. I suppose I'll kill them if it's that or be killed myself. I suppose that's what war is. I'm going to try to sleep a little before dawn comes but I don't expect I'll get much. It's not quiet, and I'm having a hard time seeing the farm. I can see Ruby, though. She's so beautiful. I love her so much. I'm glad we got married and had a couple of nights together before I had to leave. I can't wait to get home and start a family.

I'm scared. I guess the fellows at Bunker Hill were scared too. Not much to do about it now. I wish I'd told Ruby I loved her more. I wish I'd prayed more in that brick church as a kid. I wish I'd joined the Navy.

Sarge says it's time.

Moss

CHAPTER FIVE

Someone was shaking me awake out of a very, very deep sleep. I'd been dreaming about trying to drive in a snow-storm, but the images fled with the waking, leaving just a vague sense of sliding and spinning on the ice. At first I wasn't sure where I was. There weren't enough pillows for it to be Juliet's bed, and the light was coming from the wrong direction for it to be my apartment in Maryland. Whoever was doing the shaking yelled my name, the crisp sound trig-gering an unforgiving drum solo inside my skull. There was a sharp flavor to the wine hangover that I did not like at all, a million little daggers jabbing at my temples. *Stick to bour-bon,* I thought as I wrenched myself into a sitting position. Sunlight was streaming in through the glass slider, too much sunlight to hide from. Reluctantly, I opened my eyes.

"So much for seven." May was perched on the coffee ta-ble in khaki shorts and a maroon tee shirt with a picture of a hammer over the words *This Is Not a Drill.* Her prosthetic legs were strapped in place. "When it got to be seven-thirty, I figured someone needed a wakeup call." She handed me a steaming ceramic mug that smelled like slow-roasted heav-en. "Drink this, rinse off, and meet me at your car in ten minutes, sunshine. Bring an overnight bag."

I was still mostly asleep standing in cabin's little stall-shower, but as the hot water and the coffee worked their methodical resurrection, memories of the previous evening began percolating through the haze. *What was it May wanted to show me?* She had made it pretty clear that romance wasn't in the cards, and I found myself strangely at peace with that. I'd had my share of lovers, and while I was certainly attract-ed to May, I didn't feel the urgency I might have twenty years earlier. Was it maturity? Laziness? Resignation? It didn't really matter. I'd gotten a pretty clear stop sign and I wasn't interested in pushing the limits and getting rejected again. If you get thrown out at the plate, you've still had a decent trip around the basepaths. If you strike out, you go sit quietly on the bench and nurse your wounds for a while.

An overnight bag? Where was she taking me?

It was closer to twenty minutes before I made it to the car. May was leaning against the trunk of my gray Hyundai Sonata in the too-bright sunshine, her arms folded over her chest. There was a drab green duffel at her feet alongside a folded wheelchair. She raised one eyebrow and glanced at her watch.

"I know, Sergeant Pierce," I said, raising my hands in mock defense. "We're lucky I made it at all."

"Open the trunk," she said. "And it's Staff Sergeant Pierce, smartass."

I popped the trunk and she lifted the wheelchair with fluid ease. She slid it into place and then tossed her bag in alongside.

"The legs are good for around here," she said. "But I get tired after a while, and the chair comes in handy."

"I didn't say anything."

"Your face did." She opened the passenger side door and eased into the seat. "You're driving. I'll navigate. Oh," she said, with a wolfish smile, "I also get to pick the music." And she pulled the door shut behind her.

I stood there for a moment in that warm July morning, still attempting to shed the last vestiges of sleep, realizing that I was about to be kidnapped in my own car. I shook my head and drove knuckles into my eyes trying to reach the headache throbbing behind them. May was like some irresistible natural force, a tornado or an earthquake. *I'd have better luck holding my own against the tornado.* I put my own bag in the trunk and slid into the driver's seat.

We drove with the windows down, enjoying that warm, too-brief interlude between frozen mud and falling leaves when New Hampshire ascends to the pantheon of perfect places in the world. The sun was a radiant corn-yellow above, the only clouds wispy trails of spun linen clinging to the western horizon. Maples and oaks and beeches flanked the turnpike wearing their summer best, an eternity of tranquil green in every direction split by the crisp ebon strip of asphalt wandering gently northward. May wore reflective aviator sunglasses and a cryptic smile, as if half-remembering a private joke between her and the universe, raising her voice a notch above the drawled lyrics of yet another country singer caterwauling over my car's speakers. Her voice was lusty and strong yet not good, lacking in talent yet abundant in enthusiasm, a sort of atonal Janis Joplin. It had been country since the lake, songs about beer and breakups and beer and trucks and beer. I hadn't figured May for a country music fan. I'd thought more of her than that. As far as I was concerned, country was the crayon of the music family. But from her phone through my car's speakers to my ears the steady stream of twangy tragedy just kept coming, auditory hangover augmentation courtesy of May's punishing playlist.

"You like this shit?" I finally asked after about half an hour. She looked at me, expression inscrutable behind those mirrored shades. Her hair wasn't long enough to really blow wild and free behind her like in the movies, contenting itself with dancing in a frenzied blonde halo around her head.

"Six years in the Army," she replied evenly. "A good chunk of that in Afghanistan. You think it's Dartmouth grads hunting the bad guys in the caves? You either learn to like what the guys like, or you go nuts. Besides," she shrugged, "it's honest about what it is. I like that."

"I like Johnny Cash," I ventured. "And I guess Willie Nelson is okay."

"What are you, eighty?"

We drove on for a moment without talking, just listening to the songs of the South, cavalier troubadours pining for a lost love or a lost dog or a lost century.

"Are you sure it wasn't your ears they amputated?"

That earned me a smack to the back of the head.

"What did I tell you?"

"Yeah, but that was funny. And I can't imagine you're going to attack me while I'm driving."

"No. Worse." She spun the volume dial on the stereo and suddenly some good ol' boy was braying about his dying father.

"Cute," I yelled, turning it back down, thinking that maybe ear-amputation wasn't the worst idea.

"And you're buying the frappes."

"What the hell is a frappe?" I asked. The way she said it echoed how her grandmother said "crap", with a hard stop to the terminal "P" like a sudden car accident.

"A milkshake," she said, and her laugh was somehow both at me and with me all at once. "The Army didn't completely take the New Hampshire out of the girl." We were approaching the Alton traffic circle, and May pointed at the Dairy Queen. A hand-lettered white signboard out front had black letters declaring OPEN EARLY 4 SUM ER.

"Assyria and Babylon can fuck off, I guess," I said.

"You know, you're not supposed to tell dad jokes unless you have kids," May replied.

"And you're not supposed to call milkshakes 'frappes' unless you have grandkids. I've taught and coached enough to earn the dad jokes, believe me."

A few minutes later we pulled out of the drive-thru, each of us clutching an irresponsibly large paper cup. I sucked on the straw in mine and a thick chocolate slurry filled my mouth. It was cold and gritty and briefly made me feel eleven years old at the Old Saybrook seashore with my mom, getting ice cream from Honeycone and walking along the sand. It was a hot morning working on being a hotter day, and there's nothing wrong with a milkshake in the car on a day like that. I glanced over and saw that May had taken a small bottle of Ketel One out of her bag and was dispensing vodka into her strawberry shake. *Dinnertime in Kabul.*

We worked on our milkshakes and kept driving, skirting the southern edge of Lake Winnipesaukee, the grand dame of New Hampshire's lakes region. The foothills of Belknap Mountain rose to our left, and to our right the trees fell away to meet the sprawling lake. Franklin Lake was a rain puddle compared to Winnipesaukee, the crystalline blue surface stretching away and away, the distant shore a green-black smudge. Hundreds of islands dotted the water, thin white wakes from countless watercraft crisscrossing the long open stretch in the middle called The Broads. After Champlain in Vermont and Moosehead in Maine, Winnipesaukee was the third largest lake in New England, and it knew it. Along its nearly 300 twisting miles of shoreline were some of the priciest real estate in America, including the exclusive Clark Point neighborhood in the old resort town of Wolfeboro. Mitt Romney had a place there with ten or twelve bedrooms, which didn't strike me as excessive. The guy had like thirty grandchildren. In the summertime they were probably stacked up in those bedrooms like cordwood.

Along a narrow northwestern finger of Winnipesaukee called Meredith Bay we passed Weirs Beach, a little resort town that, much like Mitt Romney, had never emerged from the 1950s. A huge blue sign with the name of the town and a curving red arrow told us where to turn for the vintage plea-sures of the place. The words and arrow were bedecked by neon bulbs but they were unlit in the summer morning sun and so the sign had a mildly forlorn aspect, like a silent movie star left behind by the advent of talkies. There were other signs, smaller but no less earnest in their antique long-ing, promising soft-serve ice cream and go-kart rides and taffy. I still had plenty of milkshake, and I had never in my life been less interested in taffy. I kept driving. Our country soundtrack had blended into a kind of background blare, the milkshake or the vodka or the combination of the two merci-fully limiting May's piercing accompaniment.

Route 3 took us through rolling hills dotted with tourist trap cottage clusters. Before long there were signs for Squam Lake, and May turned down the radio torture long enough to mention that *On Golden Pond*, the Oscar-winning Hep-burn-Fonda film, had been filmed there.

"Never saw it," I said. My father had liked Katharine Hepburn. "Sexiest old broad Hollywood every produced," he once said in an interview with Johnny Carson. "Her and that minx Bacall." I wondered if he was judging based on personal experience. It wouldn't surprise me.

At Plymouth, Route 3 joined up with 93 North and we were on a proper highway again, bearing straight north as though loosed from a crossbow in anger. The state university system had an outpost up here, Plymouth State University. I was aware of it because not far to the west was Hanover and my own alma mater, Dartmouth College. I didn't know much about Plymouth State. I knew skiing and pot were majors there and students at the main campus in Durham claimed the acronym PSU stood for Piddly-Shit University. Durham kids looked down on Plymouth kids the way Hanover kids looked down on everyone. The flagship state university in Durham liked to call itself "the ivy of the publics" which is fucking hilarious, like being the hottest male server at Hooters. Might be true, but I'd never brag about it.

The highway kept on north from there, straighter than Mitt Romney, past state-owned ski areas and maple-sugar shacks and touristy pancake cabins before plunging into the White Mountains National Forest. Other than Dartmouth College and the Old Man, New Hampshire boasted a few claims to fame: the first in the nation presidential primary, Adam Sandler, and the penultimate stretch of the Appalachian Trail before it limped to its northern terminus at Katahdin in Maine. The state's share of the Trail wound somewhere nearby, cloaked by the lush carpets of spruce and fir and birch stretching summery blue-green under the cloudless sky. As we traversed Franconia Notch the cliffs rose steadily and dramatically on either side of the snaking highway. At one craggy vertical promontory May told me this was where the Old Man of the Mountain used to be until he fell some years before, a signal tragedy for both him and the people of New Hampshire. I'd known that, of course. You don't go to college in the state for four years and not get to know the Old Man. His rocky profile graces all the road signs and license plates, stone-faced and judgmental like the rest of his granite kin.

"You're like a tour guide for the past," I said. "Who's eighty now?"

"Tell me something good that's happened lately," she replied. Nothing came to mind.

You can usually smell farms before you can see them. We certainly could as we descended through the foothills on the northwest slopes of the White Mountains, the forests giving way to cropped carpets of pastureland dotted with Oreo-patterned cows who stood blithely in the morning sun. They chewed their cuds in disinterested contentment, giving no notice as my Sonata rolled past with its sore-thumb Old Man-less license plates. Their earthy, cloying fragrance was thick and unforgiving.

"Dairy cows," May said.

"Do beef cattle smell different?" I asked.

"No idea," she replied, telling me to get off the highway at Exit 37 up ahead. I had to pee, and I said as much, but May said it wasn't much farther.

"I guess I'll hold it, then."

May had been pouring vodka into her cup long since the shake had gone, but she expressed no need to visit a bathroom.

"How do you do that?" I asked. "Drink that much and never have to pee?"

"On deployment you get a college degree in not pissing," she replied with one of her enigmatic closed half-smiles. "When your legs aren't in the picture, you get your Ph.D."

We rolled into Bethlehem, a little town with prettily-painted low colonial buildings, plate-glass antique storefronts and a stodgy old brick church steeple topped with green shingles. Mount Washington and Mount Lafayette lurked with stony disinterest on the hazy horizon. It was painfully quaint, Currier and Ives porn. The downtown, with all its brief charm, didn't last long. Soon, it was cows again.

"Take your next left," May said, shifting in her seat. *Probably has to pee no matter what she says,* I thought smugly.

Outside of town the main road became a country lane, the mailboxes dwindling to intermittent grace notes punctuating the wildflower-dotted meadows that meandered down to orderly stands of pine. I could still smell the cows, but it was mixing with something sweeter, honeysuckle and straw and yesterday.

"Here it is."

This mailbox was big and brown and shaped like a barn, with an articulating red silo for a flag. The name Root was hand-painted on the side in thick white letters. Near the mailbox was a large carved wooden sign with a stylized rearing horse, declaring what lay beyond as Equinox Farm.

"This is my family's farm," May said as we drove along the hard-packed dirt road past paddocks fenced with split-rail and wire. At one point a couple of bored horses glanced at us before returning to their busy schedule of standing around near the road being vaguely picturesque. With an accompanying cloud of brown dust we parked in a cul-de-sac embraced by a rambling white clapboard farmhouse and a tidy, almost too-tidy red barn with white cross-hatchings. Two women stood looking like a Lifetime Channel reboot of American Gothic, a shaggy gray dog of moderate size and indeterminate heritage sitting between them with floppy ears and a floppier tongue. *I'm in Epcot New England,* I thought.

We got out of the car and May walked stiffly toward the taller, broader woman. They hugged like family.

"Welcome to Equinox," she said, releasing May from her burly hug and offering me a meaty hand. I shook it. It felt even meatier than it looked, like briefly holding a cooked ham. She looked nearly sixty, solid, graying, the kind of fire hydrant body that comes of a lifetime of hay and horseshit and hard winters. *Not someone to fuck with,* I decided.

"I'm Frances Root," she said, her accent a touch less pronounced than Ruby's but still magnificently provincial. "May's my niece."

"Oscar Kendall," I replied.

Frances nodded, with acknowledgement if not interest, then pointed to the woman beside her.

"My wife Erin." Erin and I nodded our hellos. While Frances was a Carhartt-clad keg of a farmer-woman, Erin was something else entirely. Trim and fit, she had a Mediterranean complexion, long black spiraling hair, and a toothy, hospitable grin. There was something collected and practiced about Erin, though not in an artificial or off-putting way. Quite the opposite, it was welcoming. I could certainly see how Frances was related to Ruby. What I couldn't quite see was how Frances and Erin had found each other. *The world can be a strange place.* Maybe opposites really do sometimes attract. Maybe the market for middle-aged lesbian lovers isn't as robust in northern New Hampshire as it is in suburban D.C. *Maybe I'm just a lonely, judgmental asshole and should let people cherish happiness wherever and however they find it.*

"And this is Ruth." I wasn't wild about dogs, but Ruth seemed harmless enough. She sat patiently, with none of the unpleasant jumping or begging for attention I generally associated with her species, cocking her head and regarding me with vague curiosity. She had a wiry steel-colored coat, a long snout, and a stubby tail that never stopped moving. She didn't bark or growl, just kept on looking. *Even the dog is a Yankee.*

"What is she?" I asked out of politeness. Every dog-owner I've ever known liked to talk about their dog. In Potomac, the canines of choice were crossbreeds involving a poodle and something else, hypoallergenic non-shedding designer mutts perfect for the exclusive zip codes near Arcadia School.

"She's a dog," Frances replied dourly. "A mongrel, like the rest of us. Walked up the drive one day and decided she liked the place. Been here four years now."

For all she seemed the central-casting reticent Yankee, Frances was a talker. She especially liked to talk about the farm. The family's ancestor Ogden Root had settled in Bethlehem before the Revolutionary War, Frances explained in her matter-of-fact tone. The property had been a hops farm in the 1700s, when New Hampshire led the world in hops production and brew-houses like Smuttynose and Frank Jones dotted the coastline like yeasty lighthouses. When the Northwest Ordinance of 1787 opened up the Territories, hops farmers fled to Michigan and Iowa and Ohio, leaving New Hampshire farms to transition to milk and cheese and apples. In the last hundred years, hops had moved west again to Oregon and Idaho. "Before long they'll be in China and Russia, like everything else." Frances snorted and spat in the dirt. I'd found the world's only Republican lesbian.

In the 1990s Frances and her partner Erin took over the farm and converted it into horse stables. Erin was an almost embarrassingly successful real estate agent across the North Country, and her commissions helped pay for Frances's horseflesh passion. Frances was the quintessential New England farmer, Erin the breadwinner

"We've got nineteen horses here," Frances said. She was voluble but her words came slowly, in their own time, like a halting spring thaw. Her delight in the farm leaked through despite her laconic attempts to mask the sin of pride. "Mostly lessons for the local kids, the occasional eventing show down in Concord or Manchester if one of the girls takes to the saddle."

"You'll stay the night, of course," Erin said with a bright smile, squeezing May's shoulder. Where Frances was a glowering storm-cloud, threatening and dark, Erin was all sunshine and the promise of good picnicking days. Erin, I liked. I wanted to like Frances too, but it would be like making friends with a rhinoceros or a Sherman tank, all thick hide with the dangerous parts staring you in the face.

"Yup. Stay," Frances grumped. "Price is a bit of help. Hay in the field needs loading."

It fell to me to pay that price, and before long I found myself sitting on the hot wooden planks of a flatbed trailer while Frances slowly towed it behind an ancient sea-green Dodge Ram pickup through the back fields. Ruth lay nearby, apparently having decided I was acceptable or else that I needed watching. Along with the horses, the modern-day Roots raised laying chickens and cultivated various subsistence vegetables alongside animal-feed crops like wheat and rye. It was hot, Dante hot, with no clouds to block the spiteful eye of the sun as Frances skillfully piloted the old truck through narrow trails and around irrigation ditches, my ass absorbing every bump and bounce. When we came to a section of field lined with rectangular hay bales tied up in twine like Christmas presents, Frances threw the Dodge into park and stumped back to meet me at the back of the trailer. I counted my teeth, surprised to find that they were all still in my head.

"Roll 'em toward you once before you pick 'em up," she said. Thickset as she was, wearing denim and long sleeves, Frances never seemed to perspire. I was already coated with a heavy rime of sweat and dirt, the proverbial whore in church.

"To get them rolling?" I asked.

"Nah," she replied. "So if there's a rattlesnake sleeping under there, the bale is between you and him."

Snakes have never bothered me much, but I have to think a lot of that is because I've tried to never bother them much.

"A lot of rattlers around here?" I asked. I think I managed to keep the tremor of fear out of my voice.

"Nah," she replied. "Snakes but nothing venomous. But it's a good habit if you find yourself humping hay out in Wyoming or someplace."

"What about Ruth?" I asked, thinking the dog might be good against any snakes, rattlers or not.

"Nah," she said again. "She ain't venomous neither."

I suspected Frances was having a bit of fun with me, but I still rolled the bales toward me as I humped. I'd never been to Wyoming, and I was content to allow that to remain the case. So I worked and I sweat, all the time mildly curious how I had found myself in a hayfield near the Vermont border alongside a butch gentlewoman farmer. May's immediate orbit seemed populated by characters who wouldn't have been out of place in an Isaiah Moss novel. Thinking of my father reminded me of his almost dogmatic disregard for manual labor. "Don't let the world make a gravedigger out of you," he wrote to me when I was thirteen.

It starts simple enough. You dig one grave, and there's ten dollars in your pocket. So you dig ten, there's a hundred. It's pretty slick when you're twenty-two and your back is strong and the shovel is light in your hands. All seduction starts with that initial transaction: you work, you get cool shit. Maybe you don't particularly like digging, but graves are paying for your bread and your broads and you like that. Before you know it, graves are paying for dresses and diapers. The corpses you bury pay the rent. You sort of hate the worms and the smell and the disrespect but you owe the bank for the mortgage and the car and college for the kids so they don't have to dig graves too. So you dig and you dig as your back breaks and your life ends and you never wrote poetry or saw the pyramids. All you did was dig your own grave.

I spent a couple of hours lifting bales of hay and tossing them onto the flatbed with Frances. There was no money, but no graves or broken backs either. Once the trailer was mostly full, she parked the old Dodge at the edge of the long hayfield, just above the banks of a slow and crooked river, mud-brown in the dry heat of July. Frances looked up at the bluebird sky and declared there'd be rain that evening. She cut the ignition and the Dodge slumped gratefully into silence.

"How can you tell?" I asked. It certainly didn't look like rain. In reply, Frances held up her smartphone, open to a radar weather application. Out of the corner of my eye, I saw a gray streak take off across the fields. Frances followed my gaze.

"Ruth," she said. "Saw a rabbit or got bored of us. She'll turn up for supper. Or she won't. I suspect that one of these days she'll move on without a forwarding address, sudden as she came."

"You seem unbothered by the idea," I observed. Frances shrugged. I liked May's shrugs better.

"Easy come, easy go. Erin's dog more than mine, though she'll come out in the fields with me time to time. She's the one that named her."

"After the Ruth in the Bible?" I asked.

"Nah," Frances snorted, "the one on the Supreme Court."

Proof of the strength of their marriage that Erin got away with that one, I thought.

"At any rate, not half bad loading for a flatlander," she said, clapping me on the shoulder with one of her five-fingered hams and regarding me coolly from beneath badger-black eyebrows and the curved brim of a Red Sox hat so weathered by sun and sweat-salt that it was more white than blue. I was relieved at the evidence that she perspired. Spiky rays of afternoon sun slanted down as Frances took a crumpled pack of Pall Malls from the glove box and offered one to me.

"No thanks," I said. "I quit a while back. If I smoke one, I'll smoke them all."

"Suit yourself. Oh, and don't tell Erin when we get back. She doesn't approve."

"Is that why we're out here? So you can smoke away from prying eyes?"

"Some things are best done that way."

We sat in silence for a minute, Frances smoking and me trying not to want to.

"So what's the story, Oscar?" she asked, looking not at me but at the smoke as it drifted out the window and away, probably hoping her wife wouldn't see it. The day was wearing on but the sun still pretended at being high in the sky with summertime delusion. The lingering smell of hay filled my nose along with the smoldering Pall Mall and my own sweat.

"What story?" I asked. The question reminded me of Juliet, though the questioner and the setting couldn't have been more different.

"Your story. Specifically, your story in relation to May."

"I'm sorry?"

"For what?"

"No, I meant I'm sorry as in I'm not sure what you're asking."

"I'm asking if you're fucking my niece, genius. Or if you're still just chasing tail."

Ah. I'd had awkward what-are-your-intentions conversations with a couple of dads back in my teen years and with one ferocious single mom. Never an aunt, and never out in the middle of a hayfield where they'd never find my body if I gave the wrong answers.

"Don't worry," I said. "We're just friends."

"Not worried." Frances took a long drag. "And bullshit."

She stared at me again. Even with the windows down the cigarette smoke filled the cab, fragrant and familiar. *Just one wouldn't hurt, right?* I swallowed that thought and stared back through the cloud with the unblinking eyes of a former veteran smoker.

"Excuse me?"

"Look," Frances sighed, blowing a double white contrail out of her nose. "I'm sure you're a perfectly swell and regular guy. But May ain't for you."

"We're friends," I protested.

"Yeah, you said. But you also wanna fuck her. I've been around enough stallions with their eye on a mare, you understand? I get it, she's an attractive girl. You should have seen her before. Like some Greek goddess. Anyway, don't do it. Find another mare."

"I appreciate you feeling protective…"

"Listen," Frances stabbed out the ruins of her cigarette on the rust of the Dodge's door and rubbed it into nothingness between a thick thumb and forefinger. "May never had a dad. Her mom, my cousin, was a real piece of work. Drugs, turning tricks, the whole bit. She died when May was two or three. Overdose. So May never had much of a mom either. It was me and Ruby who raised her, down here and up at the lake." I almost chuckled at how the terms up and down bore no relationship to north and south in the Yankee dialect, but I felt sure that if I laughed Frances might manhandle me into a cylinder and smoke me, too. "So yeah," she continued,

"I'm protective. But she's not the only one I'm trying to protect. I'm looking out for you, too"

"Me?"

"Yup. You're messing with things best left alone." Frances took off her cap, scratched at the thick bracken of tightly-curled salt-and-pepper covering her scalp, and then pointed out my window. "You see that field over there, out past the second fence, back toward the big barn? By that big spreading crimson maple? There's a track there, 400 meters around. Overgrown now, but you can still make it out if you know it's there. Exactly 400 meters, all mixed clay and ground rubber. Put it in myself when May was thirteen years old. Boy, all that girl wanted to do was run. Like a deer, Ruby liked to say, but fuck that. May was no deer. She was a cheetah, a predator. She'd run down and devour anyone in front of her like her life was at stake. I've never seen such drive. Set records over at Profile High, and the running paid the tuition at Boston College."

Frances paused, staring out the window.

"You ever run track?" she asked me. I shook my head.

"Baseball."

"OK, baseball. You ever hit a slow roller and bust your ass down the line to beat the throw?"

"More than once." Though it rarely made much difference. I had been blessed with soft hands at second and cement-mixer legs on the basepaths.

"Well, that's 90 feet of full-out. Now do it ten more times without slowing down, and that's when the piano starts to get heavy in the home stretch. The 400 meters is fifty seconds of hell on earth, and May loved it. She loved when her opponents would hit that wall down the last straightaway. They'd start to fade and I swear she'd get faster, like the agony didn't bother her. I asked her about that once, and she said it wasn't about surviving the pain, or ignoring it, but embracing it. That kid was so tough. Some days, I can still see her on that dirt track over yonder in the heat, running with dust kicking up behind her like a baby tornado. Some days, I can't see nothing else."

"I've seen amputees running with those blade things for legs," I said. "Like in the Paralympics."

"That's a great idea! Problem solved!" Frances declared, her gruff voice rising with irritated sarcasm. Then she waved a thick contemptuous hand. "You think that wasn't the first thing we tried? She won't do it. Whatever that motor was inside her won't turn over anymore. She'll swim, and she'll totter around on those dollar-store fake legs, but she won't even talk about running. She left more than her legs over in that sand. There are missing parts of her you can't just strap on a replacement for."

After another long pause, Frances cleared her throat with a choking *harrumph*.

"Dinner is chickpea burgers with sweet potato fries," she said thickly. "Erin's got this vegan thing going." She glared as if daring me to wonder how one might sustain her kind of bulk on a vegan diet, and then reached into the glove box again. Instead of cigarettes, this time she brought out a brown paper bag like winos use in the movies to hide their hooch. The bag yielded up two sticks of beef jerky and a bag of pork rinds.

"Dig in, or we'll never survive," she said. "In cooler weather I stash Snickers bars in there, but they'd turn to baby shit in this heat. At least there'll be beers at the house. Beer is vegan, thank Christ."

We both laughed at that and bit into the jerky. Frances Root had a good laugh, friendlier than the rest of her. The thick fleshy folds around her small eyes crinkled and her jowls quaked with mirth like an oversized basset hound, banishing her perpetual stormclouds for a moment and letting some sunlight into her overcast temperament. *What has this woman done with Frances?*

"Well, consider yourself warned. About dinner and about May. Felt only fair to tell you. I told you how tough she used to be. Still can be, sometimes. And yeah, I told you to watch your ass, but I'm not really all that concerned about what happens to you. She's the one I care about. Don't you fucking hurt her, you understand me? Maybe you're curious or you've got some messed-up fetish or maybe you're just some mid-life crisis pussy hunter, out the door once you get your rocks off."

"We're just friends," I tried to say again, but Frances wasn't having it.

"I ain't finished, so you shut your mouth. You're a big boy and I'm sure what some old bull dyke tells you probably doesn't matter much, but she's been through enough, you understand me? So don't you give her some taste of hope and then take it away. Don't you do it. If you hurt my little girl, I'll take that goddamned jerky back the hard way. And I won't care if there are prying eyes or not."

There's Frances, I thought.

"Let's go eat some goddamn chickpeas." She cranked the ignition and the Dodge sputtered groaningly to life. It was a short but quiet ride back to the house.

Moss

CHAPTER SIX

I found May on the patio behind the farmhouse, a cement slab bordered by red-berried shrubs, hip-high and freshly pruned. An empty bird-feeder, abandoned for the summer, hung from an iron post at one corner while an open-topped charcoal grill glowed at another, giving off waves of rising heat distorting the world beyond. Wooden latticework shot through with green tendrils of ivy and dotted with dozens of soft white electric lights stretched overhead, a sylvan pergola that would have made Pan proud. As afternoon faded into a still-blue early dusk, the overall effect was beautiful but surreal, like something from one of those yuppie magazines that tells people how to design outdoor spaces to appear beautiful but surreal. *Better Homes and Jealous Neighbors*, or something like that. A magnificently large hickory tree had donated, almost certainly unwillingly, seven feet of wood for the picnic table. Rough-cut and still clinging to shaggy brown bark on its edges, the table had a deep honeyed grain brought to a fine sheen by sanding and polishing. The legs and the chairs were crafted from the flesh of the same tree. Even a literature professor could see that it was superior workmanship and couldn't have come cheap.

"Just how successful a realtor is Erin?" I asked May, who sat in her wheelchair nearby, halfway through a brown-bottled pilsner. She seemed tired and distracted. Ruth stood panting by her side, long pink tongue lolling out one side of her open mouth. May was casually scratching the animal between her oversized ears. The dog gave me a sidelong warning stare, as if admonishing me to wait my turn.

"She does okay."

"Your Aunt Frances had a lot to say this afternoon."

"My Aunt Frances talks too much," May replied.

"They seem like good people."

"You Connecticut people think you're New Englanders," she said with a little smile. "But this is New England."

Erin and Frances came out of the house. Frances had showered and changed into clean dungarees and a short-sleeved plaid polo. She looked like an oversized, reluctantly well-scrubbed schoolboy. I'd already had my own shower, sluicing off the grime and sweat, evicting stubborn blades of hay and a couple of unwelcome ticks. I was sore from work I wasn't used to, but felt strangely satisfied, like I had earned the right to sit down. Frances headed for the grill with a platter piled with what would have been hamburger patties if they weren't a lurid yellow with green spots. Erin sat across from me and handed me a beer.

"I'm sorry we don't have any whiskey or wine," she said, and it sounded like she really was. There was a bewitching quality to Erin, some undeniable warmth, that made me like and trust her immediately. I wanted to dismiss it as artificial sweetener, the practiced slickness of a professional house-seller, but if that's what it was, she was really good at it.

"It's no problem," I said, taking the beer. "Thank you." It was cold and tasted surprisingly good.

"Nothing like a beer after a day in the fields," Frances called from where she was placing the chickpea abominations over the hot cinders. "The only thing that tastes better than the first one is the third."

"You have a lovely place," I said to Erin as we sat in the hickory chairs, drinking our first beers.

"You're very kind," she said. Frances had joined us, settling with a grunt.

"How are you related to Ruby?" I asked.

"Well, my mom, Constance, was Ruby's older sister," Frances said. "The two of them were the last two Roots, daughters of Micah Root, descended direct from old Ogden. Ruby married a Pierce from town, and my mom went off and married a Burns from down Rumney way, my father."

"So where does the aunt-niece thing come from? If your mother and Ruby were sisters, doesn't that make you May's second cousin, or once removed or something?"

"I was near twenty when May was born. Aunt just seemed easier."

"If your father's name was Burns, how did you wind up with Root?"

"What are you, the FBI?" Frances snapped.

"Hey, I'm just a teacher. I ask questions for a living." My eyes made contact with hers and held on. "So what's the story, Frances?" Something flashed across her face, either irritation or grudging respect. I wanted to believe it was the latter.

"Frances and I met at Cornell," Erin replied, resting a placating hand on her wife's burly arm. "She was studying agribusiness and I was studying, well, boys mostly. When I met Frances, I changed majors." She smiled at some private memory. "We got married as soon as it became legal in New Hampshire."

"Took Root as our married name," Frances said, taking a swallow from the bottle that all but disappeared in her hand. "Only seemed right."

"My maiden name was Papazoglakis," Erin giggled. "I figure I've saved at least a year signing my name at real estate closings since we got married."

The laughter circled the table but left May untouched. Like the night before at Ruby's cabin, she remained on the periphery of the conversation, of it but seldom in it, present and yet absent. It wasn't aloofness, or some snooty bitchiness with its judgment and its superiority. It was sadder, more divorced. Something was broken inside her.

When the chickpea burgers made their way to the table, I was skeptical, but they weren't completely terrible. They were inoffensive, like a middle of the road formula comedy or a Nicholas Sparks novel. I thought I knew what my father would have to say about veganism, but he'd been silent on the topic. I suspect he'd never encountered the word. With enough ketchup, the sweet potato fries tasted like ketchup. At one point when Erin was in the kitchen, I asked Frances if potatoes weren't vegan enough. She just shook her head in resignation.

The sun was sinking in the sky, suffusing the western clouds with a warm tangerine glow and crickets chirped blithely in the gathering dark as we finished our dinner. Erin began to clear the table, Frances staring at her beer and May lost in her own thoughts, a phantom, a photographic negative. I went inside to help with the dishes. It felt less complicated than the patio, less demanding of an emotional strength I lacked. This was a family with an open wound, and I was a stranger in their midst, a stranger threatening to derail whatever uneasy progress they'd made. Washing some plates was easier than navigating that fraught wilderness.

I swiftly learned that Erin had very particular opinions about loading the dishwasher, so my help consisted mainly of keeping her company while she did it. It was a gorgeous old farmhouse kitchen, lovingly redone, with hanging copper pots and custom cedar countertops and blue-stenciled ceramic tile backsplashes. The house and Erin Root (née Papazoglakis) were of a kind, cultivated like English gardens, a politician's focus group-tested sound bite, painstakingly curated for maximum appeal. I should have felt manipulated, but instead I was enchanted. Maybe it was an illusion, but it was a pleasant one, an unobtrusive cinnamon candle in the corner, cookies in the oven. When the dishwasher was full and churning merrily with its task, Erin dried her hands on a towel and touched my arm, just above the elbow.

"It was good of you to go with Frances today."

"I don't know that I had much of a choice," I said with grin.

"Oh, sure you did. So, thank you, again. I don't like her spending so much time out there alone. She sits out there and worries, and stares at that old track. If she wasn't an atheist, I'd say she was praying."

"Maybe she is. I know plenty of atheists who pray. Mostly hitters down to their last strike," I said with a solitary chuckle.

"And she smokes and eats her snacks," Erin said, arching an eyebrow.

"Hey," I spread my hands apart, "I don't know anything about that."

"The last couple of years have been really hard," she said, and her face clouded over, though somehow it remained an open and comforting face. It was something in the way her mouth twitched up instead of down at the corners, the way her eyes always seemed like they believed everything would turn out all right. Erin leaned against the sink and stared out the kitchen window, folding her arms over her chest. "Frances spent most of the first year after...the accident trying to bring May back. We figured she'd fight to get back on her feet the way she'd always fought before. But it wasn't working. Now, Frances just tries to protect her, like a little girl. But that's not working, either. She can't protect May from herself."

I thought about those kids at the lake, about May's swift and violent lashing out, bursting free of her like an abrupt volcano. Erin looked at me as though she were torn between two warring instincts about what to do or say next.

"Oscar," she asked, "do you care about May?"

I almost said, reflexively, *of course I do*. But that seemed more like what I supposed to say than how I honestly felt.

"I don't know yet," I said instead. Something about Erin inspired candor, her gentle patience a harmonic counterpoint to her wife's brusque intimidation, duet for violin and tuba. "That's what I'm trying to figure out. I think I'd like to." She nodded with understanding and, I think, a little approval.

"Do you want to see what May was doing while you and Frances were out in the fields this afternoon?" It was my turn to nod. "Follow me," Erin said. I trailed behind her down a hallway floored with what looked like original pine boards to the east end of the venerable Root farmhouse. There was a closed door at the end of the hall.

"This is May's room," Erin told me, pausing outside. "She wanted a room on the first floor when she was younger so she could get up early and go run without waking anyone. Of course, after...after what happened, it was convenient that she was down here and not upstairs."

Erin was stalling. I had enough experience with students beating around the bush, working up the courage to tell me their homework wasn't done, or they'd missed a project deadline, to recognize it when I saw it.

"Let's see it," I said quietly.

She opened the door.

Inside was a perfectly normal bedroom, with windows looking out over the darkening fields beyond. There was an unusually low double bed with a wooden headboard against one wall, and some other furniture my eye passed over without really seeing. In the middle of the floor, resting on a circular hooked rug, was what looked like a pile of trash in a large cardboard box. I took a couple of steps closer, and details emerged from the heap. There were trophies, false-gold women running in place, snapped free of their shiny red or blue plastic bases. Most of the women were missing their legs, smashed off by a hammer or a rock. Medals were strewn amongst the violated trophies, their ribbons shredded, their faces scrawled over by black sharpie obscuring the names of track meets where they had been won. Framed pictured, framed certificates, framed newspaper articles lay in jumbled ruins, glass shattered. May's face stared up at us from the wreckage, smiling, exulting, beyond reach.

"Jesus," I muttered.

"At first," Erin said, "we had some hope, you know? Those first few months, she was recovering from surgery, hitting her initial milestones. The Wounded Warrior guys came around. Lots of attention. Then after a while the sympathy cards and the concerned emails tapered to nothing. And she was left alone with a useless Purple Heart and an endless road ahead of her, a new reality she wanted no part of. It's like when everyone goes home after the funeral and you're by yourself in the house with a hole in your life no casseroles in the freezer can fill."

Erin stood next to me, moist-eyed, hugging herself.

"She used to spend hours in here, staring at all of this stuff. We thought it was helping, that she was coming to terms with it. I think it just made it worse. I'm used to the tantrums, Oscar. The rages. This is different. This is…"

I looked again at the pictures. It was systematic. May had smashed the glass where her own face appeared in every picture. Even when she was among several others, in team shots or competition stills, the broken glass radiated out from her face.

"Clinical," I said.

"She won't go to physical therapy. She won't go talk with anyone. She drinks all the time. Frances thinks we can just build a wall around her, but all that does is wall her in."

"That'll do."

It was Frances, filling the doorway like a plug in a tub drain, blocking the hallway light, casting her massive shadow over us both like an unwelcome blanket. Her mouth was a hard dark line of reprimand.

"Erin, this is none of his business."

"Maybe he can help her," Erin said, her voice tremulous and drained. I could feel the tension between them like a downed power line crackling on the asphalt after a windstorm. This was an old disagreement between them, one that they couldn't resolve, one that my being in the middle of did nothing to help. There was strain, but there was strength, too, a humming undercurrent of the respect and love they still shared. I'd read that when parents lose a child, it can destroy the marriage. They weren't really May's parents, and they hadn't really lost her – or had they? Their relationship looked like it was holding on, but who can hold on forever?

"She has all the help she needs," Frances replied evenly.

I dropped the framed picture I'd been holding back into the box with a thump and the soft tinkling of broken glass.

"Yeah," I said, "you're doing a hell of a job."

I thought Frances would yell, or maybe even put her hands on me, but instead she just shook her head and scowled.

"You really and truly have no earthly idea what you're talking about," she pronounced with a judge's air of finality.

"Look, May sent me to find you. Wants you to take her out in the yard for a stroll. Says to bring a beer." She squinted at me in a way that seemed intended to remind of our earlier conversation. What it really did was sharply reinforce her genetic connection to Ruby. "Mind the weather. Rain won't be long coming."

"Thank you for showing me this," I said to Erin. She was so petite and Frances was so big, giving off waves of displeasure like radiation. Then I remembered that Erin had banished cigarettes and meat from her house and figured she knew how to handle herself. Besides, I just couldn't see Frances ever hurting her. I hoped I was right.

Frances stepped aside to let me pass through the doorway, but she grabbed my arm on my way by. Her grip was strong, but not painful, not intended to hurt or even to scare. She was tall and broad but I was an inch or two above six feet myself, so I could look her in the eye.

"Oscar," she began, but I yanked my arm free.

"I'm a big boy, remember?"

I took two Vermont microbrews from the kitchen fridge and went back out onto the patio. There was a barely audible low growl of thunder, the kind of sound you feel more than you hear, picked up by some ancient prehistoric survival radar. May was sitting in her wheelchair with her back to the house, her shadow slanting long and distended in the waning moments of the day. Her head was turned in profile, sharply defined as always, blond hair cropped but softer somehow in that backlit sepia haze. She was just sort of gazing off in the distance. I wondered if, like Frances, she was seeing herself running on the dirt track her aunt had laid down for her decades before. I wondered if she could feel her legs under her, feel the wind in her face as she sprinted, feel the paired anguish and exultation of her lungs afire, her heart its own thunder. My father had eighty-seven years of the things he loved, while May's great passion had been stripped from her far too soon. If I knew what it was to love, I might have understood.

I handed her the beer, and she smiled at me in a way that made my chest tighten.

May was a holy mess, that much was obvious. The screaming at the kids, the obliteration of her athletic past, the drinking. I stared at the bottle in my hand. *What the hell am I doing?* Maybe it was May's disinterest in me that stoked my interest in her. Maybe the portrait of forbidden fruit Frances had painted only served to fan the flames. Maybe it was her being broken that attracted me, the way my being broken had attracted Juliet. *Juliet, if you'd made me feel this way, I would never have left Maryland. I'd have FedExed my dad's ashes north, curled up deeper in those unnerving gardening kittens, and died happy.*

"Push me," she said. "Just for a bit. I know it's going to rain, but we should have a few minutes." She touched my hand. "Please." It was a word I didn't think she knew. It was a word I couldn't refuse.

I jammed my own warming and forgotten beer into a pocket of my shorts and pushed. It was slow going. The tires of her chair had been made for sidewalks, not lawns. It was a little better when we reached a dirt path, winding alongside a narrow black brook where frogs chanted their good nights to each other in the mud. We were pulled along, as if drawn by some unspoken gravity, the only noise pebbles under tires and the frogs. When I saw the big crimson maple emerge, carved in graven black against the gray chalk of the sky, I knew where we were going.

The four-laned track had been partially reclaimed by the natural world, weedy greens and a hint of moss bristling the surface like unshaven whiskers. My first thought was that more should have grown in over the years since May was a collegiate runner, but then it occurred to me that Frances must have continued to maintain the track, just in case her niece wanted a place to work out when she came home to the farm. It was only over the last year, since May's injury, that it had been left to grow fallow. Thunder rolled, still far off but getting closer. Clouds had begun to gather, dark shadows against a dark sky, hiding the precocious stars that had begun to arrive.

"We should probably head back," I said. I tried to keep my voice low, but it was the pealing of a church bell in that muggy stillness. Even so, I don't think May heard me. There was no wind, the huge maple standing benevolent sentry, broad unmoving leaves more black than crimson. The oppressive humidity gathered closer and closer, the very air itself holding its breath. A storm was coming.

"This is the starting line," she said as we left the path, pushing out onto the track. Even with the encroaching vegetation, it was clear that Frances had done a first-rate job of it. *Mixed clay and ground rubber,* she had told me that afternoon. No wonder the weeds hadn't won, at least not yet. You could still see the lines, white but fading, dividing the sweeping arc into lanes. The start was staggered, with the outermost lane farthest ahead on the curve.

"Lane three."

Dutifully, I moved us to the third lane from the middle. The pale outline of a blocky numeral 3 stared up at us.

"This was my lane," May said. She twisted in her seat, looking back at me. Her hazel eyes caught what was left of the light and responded with a fire of their own, a fierce and unquenchable need. It was an echo of the faces I'd just seen in her room, faces of ferocity and hope buried under angry spiderwebs of shattered glass.

"Push me, Oscar."

I pushed. Some instinct told me to stay inside the lines, a preschooler with a crayon and a coloring book. As I walked, May leaned forward and put her hands on the wheels, shoving down on them, adding that thrust to mine. It started to get hard to keep up just walking, so I broke into an ungainly trot. The bottle of beer in my pocket was getting in the way, so I yanked it out and tossed it off into the unimportant, unreal world outside the track.

"Push," she said urgently. "We're only at the first hundred meters." Her hands flew on the tires, the toned muscles of her arms blurred circles. "Faster."

Any faster and I'd be running. The handles of the chair began to creep ahead of me, slipping out of my sweat-slicked hands. So I began to run.

"Two hundred meters," she called with a slight pant. *From exertion or excitement, who could tell?* "Faster."

We were getting to the point where faster wasn't a gear I had. After a few seconds I was at full speed. Full speed hadn't been an impressive velocity in my prime, and my prime was getting further ago all the time. Still, I begged my legs for more. I felt the sharp stab of a stitch in my ribs and ignored it. It was dark now, full dark, but I could still see the lines of lane three. There was only lane three, stretching out ahead like the nighttime road lit solely by your headlights. There was only lane three. And May.

"Three hundred," she barked, breathing hard. Her hands were moving almost faster than I could see. I began to worry that she might catch a finger or a whole hand in the flying spokes of the wheels as they spun, but she either didn't notice or didn't care. "Faster!"

Faster? It was asking a Toyota to be a Testarossa, but I reached down into wells long since dry and squeezed one last ounce of juice out of my screaming legs. Up ahead I could see a broad white band across all four lanes. A finish line, a promised land.

One of May's wheels struck a good-sized rock, and her chair swerved crazily, flinging May in one direction and me in the other. I hit the deck hard on one shoulder, trying to roll with the impact as best I could. I could hear the chair bouncing with metallic clangs against the hard-packed track, and a scream came from the darkness beyond. May, screaming more in rage than pain. I came to a stop on my hands and knees, scraped but not really hurt. The world was coming back into view, expanding beyond the narrow tunnel of lane three. Up ahead I could see the chair on one side, top wheel spinning furiously. Nearby was May, crumpled in a heap. Ten feet past her was the finish line.

I pushed myself up to my feet. My body was already sore from the hay-humping that afternoon, and now I'd just run my first – *and last,* I promised myself – 400 meters. *Well, most of it.* I shuffled achingly over to May.

"Come on," I said.

She didn't move. I wondered if she was badly injured. Putting a hand on her shoulder, I realized we were both completely drenched. Thunder boomed, closer, always closer.

"May, come on," I said. She opened her eyes and looked at me, and the look was pain and pleading. So much of what she wanted, what she needed, I would never be able to give her. But I could give her this. I put my hands under her armpits and lifted her off the ground into an awkward embrace. Reaching around my neck, she locked her arms and held on, her torso glued to mine by sweat. I didn't think about that, about her closeness, about the way our bodies were grinding against one another. All I thought about was ten more feet.

Screw you, Frances.

~~~

The distant warning grumbles had made good time, and rolling percussion now boomed directly overhead as the oppressive heat of the afternoon got ready to yield to a classic summer thunderstorm. The advance guard of fat globular raindrops began to tumble from the sky like overripe peaches, and we fled into the horse barn, the wheels of May's chair crunching on the dry straw inside. Not thirty seconds after we took cover, the sky fell down in a wet apocalypse.

May rolled to a stop alongside a rough wooden bench and swung herself stiffly over to sit on it. She hunched down a little, her customary ramrod posture reduced somehow, hands by her sides and eyes downcast. Other than a raspberry scrape on her left thigh, she seemed largely unhurt from our high-speed tumble on the track, but she hadn't spoken since we fell. After carrying her across the finish line, both of us out of breath, I had gotten her back into her chair. The damn thing was every bit the tough customer she was, and it seemed none the worse for the crash. She hadn't said anything, or looked at me, just sort of lost in her own world as we hurried into the barn. I found a switch by the door and when I flipped it a string of lanterns hanging from a central rafter flickered and came to life, bathing the main area of the barn in pools of placid gold. A horse whickered once and went back to what she was doing. May's yellow hair hung lank and wet, her face damp from sweat and the first drops of rain, glowing in the soft light with a kind of pastel radiance. It made her casually, almost innocently beautiful, ethereal and yet undeniably material, a pearl earring away from a Vermeer.

"Your father had a gun in that cabin," May said, abruptly, and the Dutch-master oil fantasy evaporated. "A Colt M1911, .45-caliber. I think it was actually the same service sidearm he had in Korea. It certainly looked like it. A nice piece, too, the M1911. Browning design, single action, semi-auto, short recoil. Even after the Army replaced it with the Beretta M9 in '86, soldiers kept using it. Hell, some of the Special Forces guys still carry them today. I carried a Beretta myself." While she spoke, she straightened back to her usual carriage and bearing, as though the words were a balm in her mouth, a psychological time machine, a martial catechism. *Why is she telling me this?* It was hot in the barn, the sweltering closeness of old wood and large animals, the occasional contented neigh or skittering mouse in the loft overhead, accompanied by the steady drumbeat of rain on the shingled roof. The leather tack hanging on the walls smelled of another time. I sat on a separate bench, a few feet away, and listened.

"The cancer was back." May was massaging her legs while she talked, digging the heels of her hands into the tops and sides of her thighs with automatic post-race muscle memory. "And I think he was in a lot of pain."

"The gun," I said. "Did you think he might..?"

"Off himself? Nah. He did make me promise one day that if the pain got too bad, I'd put him down like a blown horse. 'Eat your own damn bullet,' I told him, 'you were a soldier, for Chrissakes.' 'A long time ago,' he said. 'And I was a lousy shot.'" Anyway, he enjoyed life too much, I think. 'I love mornings,' he used to tell me. 'Each day has such potential. You could write the best sentence of your life. You could get laid.' I don't think you check out unless you've given up on those possibilities, and from what I could tell, your old man never did. I'd see him in the morning, bringing beers to the dock after my swim. 'Another day?' I'd ask. 'Another page, another pussy,' he'd answer. I don't think there was much of either the last few years, but he kept saying it."

You'd be surprised, I thought, thinking of the manuscript in the cabin, and maybe of Ruby too.

"That doesn't make a ton of sense to me," I said. "He didn't want to kill himself, but he was OK if you did it?"

"I think he felt that if he had it together enough to load and fire a gun, he had enough marbles left to write and maybe screw. Once that was gone, once his faculties had eroded and the possibilities with it, he wanted someone to handle it for him." She ran her hands through her damp, matted hair, and slow rivulets of water tumbled lazily down the back of her neck. "And I think maybe he just didn't want to be alone at the end."

In the quiet that followed, I could hear a subtle, papery whispering nearby. Something long and sinuous was winding through the loose straw on the floor, just a few yards away and moving in my direction. In a heartbeat I moved to join May on her bench, pulling my feet up in front of me.

"Jesus, Kendall, it's a garter snake."

"Yeah, but I don't have a hay bale."

"What?"

"Never mind."

The loudest boom yet shook the old wooden rafters, as sheets of rain kept falling outside. Behind those curtains of water, inside the wooden bivouac of the barn, I sat next to May on that rough-hewn bench, so far from anything I had ever dreamed, ever wanted, ever considered. I reached across my body and hers with my left hand and placed it on her right hip, a knowing, intimate gesture.

She plucked my hand off with one of her own.

"I don't need your charity," she said.

I folded my hand back into my own lap.

"Like I'm charitable," I replied. "May, are you okay?"

"I'm a runner with no legs, Oscar. No, I'm not fucking okay."

"I meant..."

"I know what you meant," she said. Her bronze eyes locked on me. "Not my first bumps and bruises. By the way, thanks for my last lap."

"My last too, I think," I said with a chuckle.

There was nothing then between us for long minutes except for the thunder and the rain.

"I saw the stuff in your room," I said finally, unable to leave it alone. May waved a hand.

"I don't need that stuff anymore," she said. "Time to cut ties, am I right? Enough is enough."

I chewed on that for a minute. When my ex-wife left me, I threw away the letters and cards she'd sent me, pictures, gifts, anything that reminded me of her. Closure. Moving on. Maybe that was what May needed to do with her own past.

"Do you want to know what happened?" she asked quietly.

I was no therapist. I was just some guy from the next cabin at the lake. But if talking to me helped, that was fine with me. Besides, I was curious.

"Sure."

"I'd finished college," she said, "and I wasn't good enough to be a professional runner, so I needed to do something. I ended up joining the Army. Could have gone to officer training school, but I wanted to be a medic. I'd majored in biology at BC and spent enough time in the trainer's room with running injuries to know my way around some sports medicine, so I thought that was the way to go. Summer of 2013 I headed overseas with my unit. Initially, we were just outside of Jalalabad in eastern Afghanistan. Man, it was a wild time."

"That must have been awful," I murmured sympathetically. May looked at me as though no one had ever said anything half so crazy.

"I loved it," she said. "I was out in the field more often than not, patching guys up. Sometimes back in the FOB training or cycling off forward duty, but mostly outside the line. Patrolling, recon." There was a glitter in her hazel eyes, the memory of fulfilment, the memory of life. "The shit we were doing mattered. Even the silly hearts-and-minds crap in the villages, handing out candy to kids and milk to single moms whose husbands died shooting at us the week before. Six years I was there, playing capture the flag with the warlords, and we were winning."

Again minutes stretched with just the thunder and the rain. This time, I knew enough not to talk.

"God, I loved it," she repeated. "My work, my teammates. And I was running too, not the 400, not anymore, but road running, distance stuff. A buddy turned me on to marathons a couple of years out of school, and it was the shittiest joy ever, three hours of shitty joy. I was hooked. Did okay in some of the enlisted competitions, but it was never about the hardware, just about the hard. Life was good."

More minutes. More thunder, right above and around us, flashes of sudden white turning the darkling barn to noontime. Rain pounded, and pounded, but I couldn't hear it.

"About two years ago," she continued, and I couldn't tell if she was talking to me, to herself, or if she had no idea that she was even talking instead of just remembering, "we were in the Tarinkot District, in a shit-ass little village called Sar Shekli along the Bamiyan-Kandahar Highway, right in central Afghanistan, right in the fucking guts of it. We were meet-and-greet corps with the locals. Kissing hands, shaking babies, the whole thing. A kid comes my way, maybe five years old. Cute thing. Big black eyes, skin like sandalwood, chubby little fingers. I give her a Snickers bar, and she moves her hands out wide like she's going to give me a hug. I go down on one knee and that's when I see it."

May paused, and the instincts within me wavered between biting my tongue, urging her to continue, and reaching out a comforting hand. I elected to sit there. It was my default choice, doing nothing, letting the world unfold as if I had never been. *Better to be ignored than reviled. Better to dare nothing and fail nothing.* The kid who tore the cover off the ball in the summer of '92 had learned that there was no such thing as a good pitch to hit any more.

Eventually, reverie become recollection and May continued.

"She had an improvised explosive device strapped to her midsection," she said. "I tried to pivot away, but she grabbed my leg and held on like a barnacle. I couldn't get away. It was like my leg was in a bear trap. I was looking right in her face when the fucking thing went off. She wasn't even crying. Thankfully the thing was a piece of crap. If it had been a professional job, I'd have been a red wet stain on the sand. As it was, it tore up my legs. They airlifted me to Bagram, or so they tell me. I don't remember any of it. The docs took everything from just above the knee and saved my life."

May looked at me then, right in the eye, and I realized she'd been utterly present the entire time, that she'd been telling me this story, not engaging in some twisted kind of reflection.

"Honestly, all I can remember is that little girl, holding her Snickers bar in one hand while she hugged my leg, trying to kill me. When I say I can't have kids, Oscar, it's not because my body won't do it or because there isn't a mom somewhere in my soul. It's because every time I see a toddler at the park or a kid holding their grandfather's hand at the mall, I want to run away as fast as I can, or draw the weapon I don't have and kill them. Because I want to scream at my guys to get away. When I say I don't like kids, it's because they scare the shit out of me more than any goddamn snake."

How do you respond to a story like that? I thought about May's reaction to the Wheeler children playing in the water at the lake, about how uncomfortable she'd been the entire time they'd been there, how the terror and trauma must have been building in her, barely controlled, a dam weakening until it burst. I pictured the brutalized artifacts of May's past piled up in that box, unwanted talismans of a past too painful to contemplate. And I thought of all those notebooks in my mother's basement. *If I couldn't write anymore, would I keep them? Would I surround myself with jeering reminders of my eviction from Eden?* I put my arm around her, because I didn't know what else to do. Instead of pushing away she leaned in, her head tilting onto my shoulder. I stroked her bare shoulder lightly with the thumb and forefinger of my right hand, willing comfort, willing healing, willing anything I had that might help. I felt her head move just a trifle, her spiky blond hair tickling the skin of my neck. I glanced down. May was looking up at me, the depthless grief in her eyes more than I could stand. With no other emotional clubs in my bag, I kissed her.

For a flickering instant May responded, her lips crushing against mine with a frantic hunger. Then she broke free, shaking her head. She took one of my hands in both of hers and held on as though for life itself.

"Oscar," she whispered, "I need a friend, too."

~~~

I laid awake that night in the farmhouse guest room long after the others had gone to sleep. It was a cute little room, clearly old like the rest of the house but the fortunate recipient of Erin's deft decorating touch. The walls were painted a clean shade just a touch creamier than pure white, with forest-green trim that matched the speckled-green patchwork of the summer quilt on the bed. The pillows had chickens on them, but they were just chickens. None of them were driving tractors or wearing overalls, which I appreciated. The windows were open a little and I could hear the rain still thudding down outside. A frog-strangler, Frances had called it when May and I came back to the house, sodden and oddly sheepish, as though we were teenagers who had stayed out past curfew. Frances didn't say much, just commented in passing on the storm and handed us towels. May rolled to her first-floor room without another word, just a small look and small smile in my direction. I wondered if Erin had cleaned up the mess there. I had to bet she did. *This is a woman who starts doing the dishes while people are still eating.* Frances showed me up a narrow stairwell with uneven stairs to the chicken-pillow room. She didn't smile, but she also didn't retrieve any jerky.

My body was sore and exhausted, but sleep wouldn't come. I couldn't stop seeing May and the little girl and the bomb. I couldn't stop picturing her running and jumping and swimming, young and whole and alive. I couldn't stop hearing the catch in her voice, the desperation, when she said my name in the barn. She was in so much pain, and I had no clue how to help her. *Maybe just give her what she asked for. Be her friend.* I wasn't sure if I knew how to do that.

~~~

Breakfast was oatmeal with soy milk and bananas. I was certain Frances thought about bacon the whole time. I know I did. After we packed our stuff into my car, Erin enfolded both May and me with long hugs. She smelled like fresh-sliced watermelon, clean and good.

"Come back and see us anytime," she said, mostly to May. "And for longer."

Frances gave May an enveloping hug that lasted even longer than Erin's, whispering something in her ear. She didn't hug me, but she did shake my hand again.

"Take care," she grunted. *Of her* was unspoken but obvious. She smelled like New Hampshire. I glanced around, but Ruth hadn't bothered to show up to say goodbye. *The life of a farm dog must be a busy one.* Or else maybe she'd finally moved on.

We got in my car and headed south.

Moss

The rain had stopped sometime before dawn and the world felt new, the sins of the night washed clean and a new day unfolding with equal parts promise and peril. The sun grinned down on us bright but not hot, just a few straggling puffy clouds scudding eastward in a fresh breeze. May and I talked about things that didn't matter as we drove, retracing our steps south to the lake. It was as though what had happened last night tore free the scab guarding a still-healing wound. While the exposure to the air was probably good for it, it was still fresh, something you didn't want to pick at or even look at too closely. So we talked about the weather, or the Red Sox, or restaurants. At one point, May opened an orange and blue soda can she'd gotten from the garage at the farm.

"What is that?" I asked.

"Moxie," May replied.

"Never heard of it."

"You wouldn't like it," she said.

"Try me."

With a half-shrug and the hint of a smile, she handed me the can, and I took a investigatory sip. I promptly spit it out the window.

"I tried to warn you."

"It tastes like root beer having a mid-life crisis."

"It's an acquired taste," she said from behind her aviators. "It's not for everyone."

May fell asleep somewhere between Thornton and Campton, her head resting on a balled-up white fleece against the window, her breathing even and untroubled. Her tattoo peeked out over the neckline of her ribbed canary top, even the bird seeming to relax in its cage. The radio still played, more of her country music. I turned it down, but not off. It didn't seem to bother me quite so much now.

CHAPTER SEVEN

Their wartime service was one connection between Isaiah Moss and May Pierce, a shared language I might be able to understand but never speak with any fluency or authenticity. May's ferocity on that rural track hinted at another. My father, improbably, was a sports fan. As much as he enjoyed his relationships with fellow writers like Hemingway and Vidal, he also leveraged his new celebrity to cultivate friendships with athletic heroes like Namath and Ali. He liked large personalities and excellence, and as his literary star began to rise, he could be found rubbing shoulders with movie stars and athletes. There was a picture in LIFE magazine in 1958 or '59 at Toots Shor's Manhattan watering hole, Isaiah Moss between Marilyn Monroe and Mickey Mantle, laughs and cocktails and eternal youth. He loved his buddy Mantle and he loved the Yankees because they won, and because they had style. I also think Isaiah Moss and Mickey Mantle understood each other.

Mantle was all a man should aspire to be. Young, drunk, worshipped. You never saw him play. You watch these prim modern greyhounds, all diet gurus and specialized workouts, hothouse flowers, all of them. The Mick was no orchid. He was a fucking weed that took seed in the Oklahoma sandlots and fought through locusts and tornados to become Mickey goddamn Mantle. He was a bumpkin, a redneck with a Biblical swing and a cannon on his shoulder. Mantle fucked pitchers the way DiMaggio fucked Monroe. His father was a zinc miner. You don't want to mine zinc, you'd better hit the ball. My dad was a dairyman before the War. He drove the coastal route in Toms River, Cranmoor Drive and Hooper Avenue and Fischer Boulevard before the New Jersey dawn, leaving bottles on the doorsteps of our more well-to-do neighbors. There was an oyster warehouse on his route, a sprawling wooden depot where single women shucked the shellfish men dredged from Barnegat Bay. Every day for a thousand years my old man left a dozen glass quart-bottles of whole milk from the Clover

Dairy Farm along with some butter at the concrete front stoop of that oyster warehouse under the shadow of a gothic brick façade. One day he was home after his shift when the supervisor at Clover called. It seemed the warehouse had burned down in the night, leaving just that façade. Who could tell in the pre-dawn? My father had delivered milk to a place that wasn't there. Milk was fifty cents a gallon and gas only twenty, so he had to drive back out there and fetch it. I didn't want to deliver milk any more than the Mick wanted to mine zinc, but I couldn't hit a curveball, so it was Korea for me, and words. Words were my life raft, my fire escape, my disgustingly wealthy widow mistress. Words saved me from a life of labor. Is it any wonder why I love them?

They say Mantle drank too much. You bet he did. Boy, some people drink because they fail. Others drink because they can't fail. The world expected him to hit a home run every time he walked to the plate. Every swing he took that wasn't a round-tripper wasn't good enough. You'd drink, too.

As much as my father enjoyed sports, cherished them as a substitute for more high-stakes aggression, he lacked patience with the perpetual epidemic of well-coiffed microphone jockeys describing the action on the field in terms better suited to a breathless Pentagon jock-carrier. He wrote an article in The Sporting News in 1991, when Gulf War rhetoric had seeped into every cranny of national discourse and the martial allegory of sports talk was at its masturbatory apex.

The beauty of athletic endeavor – professional, amateur, scholastic, sandlot – is that a boy can strike another boy with savage malice in demonstration of his masculine prowess, under mutually agreed-upon rules, and one boy – or, in a team sport, a group of boys, a tribe of boys – will be victorious. Male ego and male curiosity and male honor is satisfied, with precious few grieving widows. I say boys because sports are played by boys, and never men. What of girls, you ask, and women? Yes, they frolic in the fields too, but there is an absence of warlike intention, of barbarism for its own sake in their play, and that is the essential point here.

Boys (and girls and women, I suppose) throw a ball while men shoot guns. Men fight wars, and that is our tragic idiocy.

That idiocy, that tragedy, is comprehensible, perhaps even inevitable, as it almost always arises from committees of wealthy men organized and presided over by wealthier men bearing titles with words like Security and Defense, ludicrous titles as their actions universally arise from insecurity and are nearly always indefensible. They are motivated most often by profit, and sometimes by ideology, which is less excusable than profit in that one cannot spend ideology on cocktails or women or cocktails for women. Greed, at least, while bilious, is fungible.

What cannot be sanctioned is the sportscaster in his screen-tested navy blazer and lacquered hair intoning with mid-American inoffensiveness that a player is "in the trenches" or "under fire" or "rallying the troops". When a fullback's failed block kills his entire team, when a point guard's errant pass mistakenly vaporizes a civilian target, when a shortstop's booted grounder sends shrapnel into the flesh of the third baseman, then you may make free with the battlefield similes. Until then, use that time giving us the score more often, especially on the radio.

What offends about such misplaced language? Do I find it insulting to the memory of slain men I knew and marched alongside who will not watch this year's Super Bowl surrounded by guacamole and grandchildren? Does it cheapen the blood sacrifices of American youth who even now stand between America and our chosen enemies with a flag on their sleeve and a gun in their hands while patriotic cowards wave flags from their bivouacs of comfort? Yes, and yes. And yet, the worst of it is that the language of warfare infiltrates the gridiron and the playground and the political debate-hall, and we make things that are not war into war even as we labor to make war less warlike with our targeting computers and our unmanned drone strikes and our atmospheric missiles. We've transmuted war into a sanitized game, played by fighter pilots a thousand miles away from enemy lines who have never left the ground. We have automated and minimized the human cost of war. War has become less terrible, and so it is easier to compare other less terrible things to war.

You will, reader, laugh at such commentary from an old man whose fighting days are done. You will reject these concerns as the hand-wringing of a grandmotherly veteran out of touch with the modern age. You will dismiss sports-as-war analogies as mere words, harmless wind. In response I will simply say that words are my business, dear reader. They aren't paying you a tidy sum for your thoughts on this topic (or any other, I suspect). I am an expert where words are concerned. In the field of words I am a brain surgeon, a rocket scientist, a multiple Cy Young winner. So listen when I tell you that words matter. Language matters. It changes how we think and how we act, or at least it should. This is what separates us from the animals. Though I am forced to wonder if some of us are more separate than others.

Isaiah Moss was not a pacifist, but he despised war. He loathed it in the way only those who have seen war can loathe it. It was a personal hatred. He hated war as much as he loved sports. I think he didn't want to see the purity of the one contaminated with the rot of the other. And it was almost never a political consideration for him, at least not in the sense that one party or candidate was any better than another. I don't recall him ever publicly supporting anyone. He liked Kennedy, but that was because the man had style. He called Democrats "sad solvers" and Republicans "hoary hoarders" and disdained them both. "They're all leeches," he wrote me once in regard to one upcoming election. "They all get fat on blood." He was an ideological agnostic. I wouldn't be surprised if he never voted for anyone.

I was a pretty decent baseball player myself, back in the Little League years when managers were disinterested dads with a cigarette butt hanging from their bottom lip, napping at the end of the bench during games. I was never afraid of the ball the way some kids were, and I liked hitting, the immediate feedback of it. Baseball is a binary exercise, a zero-sum game of success or failure. You get on, or you get out, and no lawyer will ever change your sentence. I was never quite good enough to be the shortstop. I wasn't that kid, the preternaturally rangy and long-boned twelve year-old who looked like he might have to miss a game for his driver's test, a head taller and a country mile better than the rest of us. There was a lot less acne and a lot less pressure for a second baseman, and that's where I prowled. My father never saw me play, but that didn't make me much different from my teammates. I could probably count on one hand the number of times my mother saw me play, and then probably not until high school. I invariably rode my bike to the field, one more dented Huffy leaning against the outfield fence with all the rest. Mine was royal blue, with a Ryne Sandberg baseball card tucked into the spokes of the back wheel. I was a Connecticut kid, inhabiting the demilitarized zone between Red Sox nation and the Yankee empire, but Ryno was my guy, a Chicago Cub, a glove man with some pop who could turn two slicker than snot on a doorknob.

We were children of the Eighties, the last of the free-range suburban kids, before media-fueled fears of child abduction, before parachute parents and self-esteem curricula and the sneaking suspicion that a kid who could hit a ball might be mom and dad's way out of the zinc mines. Years later, at Arcadia, parents would stand there and watch my softball team practice. I can't think of anything more yawn-inducing or pathetic.

I actually enjoyed playing baseball, and I like to think it enjoyed me playing it, at least for a while. It was one of the few mutually fulfilling relationships I've ever had, if only for a time, if only until I failed at that too. The crisp white uniforms with their navy pinstripes and the newly-cropped grass and the adolescent heat of June are some of my favorite memories. Baseball is one of God's birthday presents to the world, a perfect thing. There's a reason the game is played on a diamond. It's all been written about before, and by writers better than me. Baseball is America's literary pastime. There are no poems about snowboarding. We moved around a lot when I was a kid, my mom always thinking the next job the next town over would be better. Every time we moved, I had to make new friends, and baseball was usually the quickest path. Baseball is like America that way. If you can play, if you can produce, you're accepted.

I loved the game, but all love ends. The specific day when I knew my days in the sun had an expiration date came less than a year after my father's Sporting News diatribe. I was fifteen, had just finished my sophomore year in high school, and was playing summer pony league ball. We were the Cubs that year, and I was able to score number 23 for my jersey, just like Sandberg. That season I was as good as I'd ever be, getting solid wood on the ball and locking down second base like a prison warden. The slap tag, the pivot, the pickoff play, even a hidden ball trick one time. Second base is about footwork and quick hands, and at fifteen I had both with a will to use them. We played three or four games a week, under the lights at night on Tuesdays or Fridays and on weedy sun-baked infields Saturday afternoons. I remember it being hot every day that summer. It never rained, and a baseball cap was a crown. If you took Springsteen's *Glory Days* and Fogerty's crappy *Centerfield* and put them in a blender with Mellencamp's *Summer of '69*, you'd get a glassful of July 1992. (Or was *Summer of '69* by Bryan Adams? Is there a difference?) There was even a girl, Maura, a poor man's Meg Ryan in cuffed denim shorts, cute more than pretty, flirty more than ready. We made out a few times, she let me touch her under the bra one night in the woods behind the Essex fairgrounds. Man, I was a second baseman to be reckoned with that summer.

Our Cubs made the playoffs, and while we knew we lacked the horses to win it all we were enjoying the ride. I will never forget what our coach, Mr. Watkins, told us. "Maybe you're not the prettiest girl at the dance. Put on your best dress, show up and maybe you get lucky when the music starts." Sometimes I wish I could repeat that to my teams, but it's not 1992 anymore and there are things a male coach doesn't say to his female players, including analogies about getting lucky. Not with parents at practices.

When the music started at our dance, we found ourselves playing the Cardinals from down in New London. They were the defending champs with plenty of returning players, chief among them their starting pitcher that afternoon.

Cooper Clay was eighteen and six-foot-two, easily over 200 pounds, and he actually had these defined biceps at a time none of us had biceps. Some guys used to lift weights a bit then, mostly the football players who would chant "curls for the girls", but in those pre-social media days it didn't seem all that important to carve ourselves out of marble. We were competing with the guy from down the street, not with some impossible Hollywood standard. Except Cooper Clay. He wasn't competing with anyone, because there was no one at our level who could compete with him. He just blew guys away with a fastball that flirted with 90 and a curveball that fell out of the sun. Our leadoff batter that day came back to the bench and said that the ball had laughed at him on the way past. Our number-two hitter came back advising us to start our swing while Cooper was still in his windup. Dude was chucking BBs.

I was our third hitter, and I remember it like this morning. I stepped into that batter's box with all the cockiness of teenage semi-competence. I'd seen the ball well all year, hitting damn near .400, and I figured *yeah, he's fast, but I'll time him up and get the bat on it.* When I looked out at him, I could have sworn that mound was ten feet high. It was like digging in against a guy pitching from a stepladder. And Cooper had this glare, this graven scowl, like you'd wronged him somehow and his preferred method of revenge was humiliation with a baseball. I'd never seen a face more focused, more suffused with intention of harm, or more thoroughly coated with zits.

Take the first one, I thought, willing myself not to be afraid. *Let's see what he's got.*

I did, and in my memory the pitch knocks the catcher back into the umpire and they both blow through the backstop like something on Looney Tunes. I was down a strike and I'd never even seen the pitch. The home plate umpire probably never saw it either, but it certainly sounded like a strike. Christ, it sounded like a freight train.

The second pitch was much the same. I thought of my father's Sporting News essay from the year before, the one I hadn't told anyone my father had written, and I suspected that if this wasn't war, no one had told Cooper Clay. He had a fucking Howitzer and worse, he knew it.

I wasn't going to go down looking. I had that much pride. I had caught just enough of a glimpse of that second fastball that I thought I could at least foul the next one off. Damn, the compromises we make with our standards in the pursuit of preserving ego. So I took a deep breath, and as soon as Cooper's front foot came off the ground, I began my swing. I swung hard, too – if you're going to prison, it might as well be for murder.

And that pizza-faced asshole threw me his Uncle Charlie. I could have swung twice in the time that sweeping hook spent getting to the plate, curving like a fighter jet avoiding fire. I took a cut like a lumberjack trying to get the tree down with one swing, and I lost my balance. I fell down in a heap, a jumble of arms and legs and the queasy realization that there were humans and there were gods in this game as in all games, and that I was very much not a god. It was sobering and stunning, and I've never forgotten what Coach Watkins said when I got back to the bench.

"We all meet our match, son."

The thing is, so did Cooper Clay. He wasn't a god either. Years later I read in a local newspaper that he'd been signed by the White Sox out of high school, and made it as high as Double-A, playing for the Birmingham Barons. The article in the paper was mostly about how Cooper had a locker next to Michael Jordan while the basketball immortal was flirting with a baseball career. What the article didn't mention was that Cooper's fastball wasn't live enough and his curveball not nasty enough for the major leagues. He had a Double-A arm. The guy who was way better than me wasn't nearly good enough. His lasting brush with fame was that he'd been naked next to Michael Jordan a couple of times. And that in a pony league game in Connecticut in 1992 he struck out Isaiah Moss's son three times on nine pitches. Not that anyone knew, least of all Cooper Clay, that pimply fuck.

I kept playing, but most of the joy was gone. I'd gotten the memo almost all of us get, the indisputable notification that our future will involve fewer ballfields and more zinc mines. I played high school ball my junior year, though not well. I didn't play at all as a senior, my glove in my mom's basement alongside my notebooks and my wallpaper best-sellers. I think I threw my Ryne Sandberg card away.

~~~

The lumpy, misshapen couch in the Scrotum's living room could never have been just right, not even if a whole sleuth of bears tried it, and my night at the Root family farm had reminded me how comfortable a real bed could be. So, the second week in July, I moved into my father's bedroom at the cabin.

It was sparingly furnished, less than eighty square feet, scarcely enough for the sturdy pinewood double bed and a secondhand-looking little bedside table. *Just one nightstand. Perfect.* I had to imagine that most of my father's assignations with Ruby Pierce took place in the cozier, more hospitable cabin next door. There was a lamp on the table but no clock. I hadn't seen any timepieces in the cabin; even the stove and microwave oven had read a noncommittal 0:00 when I arrived. Isaiah Moss lived by his own rules, even when it came to time. I pictured him getting up whenever he wanted and going to bed whenever he wanted and writing and drinking and fucking in between as the mood struck him. He was basically a literate, unfixed cat. There was a single paperback next to the lamp, and I glanced at the cover. Wilde's *The Picture of Dorian Gray*. I knew the book well and had taught it many times to bored sophomores. I wondered if my father regarded it as cautionary tale or personal fantasy.

A high window above the bed looked out on a copse of young white birches, greenish light trickling through into the tiny room. On the opposite wall was an accordion-style folding door that opened onto a snug closet. There was a compact dresser inside, and some clothes hanging from a suspended wooden dowel. Jackets, sweaters, nothing fancy. Isaiah Moss hadn't been a full-on clothes horse in the mold of his fellow-traveler Vidal, but he had been particular about his shirts. Always Italian-made, Armani or Brioni, always French cuff, always bespoke.

You won't know how a man should dress, he wrote to me during my years at Dartmouth, *but that's not your fault. No one does any more. Sinatra could dress. Kennedy. Poitier. Beckett thought he could dress, but he wore turtlenecks. He was also an Irishman who thought he was a Frenchman, so fuck Beckett. The French. To their credit, they gave us cuffed shirts. They also gave us Proust, which I can forgive, and a bag of shit in Southeast Asia, which I can't. Astaire. Christ, Astaire could dress. He knew you don't put soda in your booze and you wear Italian shirts. The French and the Italians, unserious people making serious clothes. People want to talk about English clothes, but the English were wearing wolf-skins on their soggy island when the Romans invented hygiene and shirts. The French and Italians make clothes the way the English make enemies.*

As a cultural historian, my father's expertise was suspect.

Beneath the dresser were two boxes. One was steel and black and had a lock on it, but the key was in the lock. It was heavy. I dragged it out and lifted the hinged top. Inside was a worn leather pouch, and inside the pouch was the gun May had mentioned. Along with the gun and pouch were a couple of boxes of ammunition. Unlike my father, I wasn't a bad shot. I had never fired a gun in my life, so there was no evidence what kind of shot I was. I had no ambition to ever find out. *Had my father fired a gun since Korea?* I put the Colt .45 back in its pouch, put the pouch back in the case, and closed the lid.

The other box was full of cufflinks.

If the Remington typewriter was the Holy Grail of Isaiah Moss, here were the splinters of the Cross. Cufflinks were serious business to my father. In a *Rolling Stone* feature from the '80s, he waxed eloquent in perhaps the longest sustained paean to cufflinks in the history of the written word.

"Buttons are for factory workers," he was quoted as saying. "Cufflinks, now, convey individualism without overt crass egotism." *When,* I wondered, *had overt crass egotism ever bothered Isaiah Moss?* "They are a simple, elegant signal of dignity, an unspoken shibboleth between cultured men." He went on for quite some time, warming to his topic. I don't how much the writer of the article or their editor took out, but they left more than enough in.

Many of mine are mementoes, souvenirs of times and places and people. Of course, once an old woman collects a few porcelain penguins, she will soon be drowning in the idiotic birds, convenient gifts each Christmas from well-meaning granddaughters and lazy husbands. Readers who know of my predilection will insist on sending me gifts. These mean nothing to me and usually end up in the trash. I have no compunction about throwing things away. Writing is deletion far more than retention. If you are so fervid in your affection, dear readers, save yourself the trouble of shopping and just send me the money.

The box was made of polished chestnut with a lid that split in two and swiveled open at four levels like a jewelry case. The molded velvet lining held dozens of pairs of cufflinks. Gold, silver, plain or adorned with embedded gemstones flickering in the light from the window. Some were engraved with his monogram, I.M. My father never used a middle name. I'm not entirely sure he had one. There were pewter sets and ivory, and what looked like deer antler. One pair was made of yellowing pearls with painted-on pheasants that had begun to flake off. *A story for each, or a memory,* I thought. I picked up another pair that was shaped like dragonflies. All stories I'd never know. Stories no one would ever know. I replaced the cufflinks as carefully as I'd replaced the pistol, and tucked the two boxes back under the dresser. Grenades should be buried in sand, as deeply as possible.

Who the hell keeps a case of cufflinks at a lake house?
Who the hell calls their lake house "The Scrotum"?

As usual, my father had his own reasons, his own rules, all of which were impenetrable to me now. If he hadn't written the answers in his books, or in his letters to me, they most likely died with him. So much brilliance lost. *So much more whiskey for the rest of us.*

Something next to the boxes caught my eye, something not quite right. One of the pine floorboards was loose. Small surprise, a place of this age and general condition. But I could see something underneath the board, something that looked like fabric. Intrigued, I put my fingers alongside the loose board and it came free with almost no effort. Underneath, in a space the size of a shoebox, was a brown canvas bag tied with a drawstring. I took it out and opened it, my hands trembling.

The bag was full of letters.

A couple were from me. I recognized the broad, juvenile script as my own. Only a couple, though. I had written my father twice. The first time, I asked for toys and got a dictionary in return. The second time, as a freshman in college, I asked for writing advice. I received back the shortest letter my father ever wrote me.

Writing isn't a question of can, his typewriter wrote me back. *It's a question of can't not.*

But there were more envelopes. Yellower, older, thicker, addressed to my father at his childhood address in Toms River, New Jersey. The seals on all of them were broken, so I opened the one with the oldest postmark, dated spring of 1943, when my father was eleven years old. I slid the folded paper out and gingerly spread it on my lap. It practically screamed at me from the past.

"Isaiah," it began, "I miss you, boy."

If I could pick anywhere on this earth to be, it would be at the ballfield watching you play. But I've got a uniform on my back, a rifle in my hands, and Nazis to fight. I'll take care of Europe, you take care of your mom. We'll whip Adolf and make the world safe, and I'll be home as soon as I can. Just a job of work to do before then. Hit the books and hit the ball and don't worry about me. I've got the Stars and Stripes on my sleeve and that flag hasn't been beat yet. Be a good boy, and I'll see you soon.

I clutched the letters in my lap, an unexpected totem of familial faith. A whole pile of them, thirty or forty missives from my grandfather to my father. A few short weeks before I'd had no sense of family, no ancestral connection, no roots. And here, on a stack of long-saved eighty-year-old paper, was a record of my father's love from his father. *The dairyman*. It felt tingly and slightly painful, like holding an electric fence. I had a past, a history, a lineage.

Sicily is warm, the second letter read, *like Virginia in the summertime. I'm tired but these are good fellows and we're ready to get at the belly of the enemy. Churchill calls it Europe's soft belly but it's not that soft. Still, Hitler's days are numbered. Boy, nothing can stand against America when we wake up and get moving. Hit a homer for me, like Joltin' Joe.*

I tried to picture my granddad as I inhaled the letters. In my mind he looked like my father but thinner, rakishly handsome, Clark Gable in drab green. He definitely had one of those pencil-thin moustaches, like Walt Disney with a twinkling eye, a ladies' man but faithful to my grandmother. I imagined him writing to her too, with her corset and pointy bra and beehive hairdo, aging but still handsome underneath all that packaging. Their song was a Glenn Miller number, Moonlight Serenade or A String of Pearls, something they had danced to before Japan surprised us at Pearl Harbor and American boys started heading to Europe and the Pacific. I imagined them as a family, with bedtime stories and trips for ice cream, the ending of *It's a Wonderful Life* complete with Zuzu's petals.

I swallowed them all at once, sitting on my father's bed in my father's bedroom. The letters read like Beadle's dime stories from an earlier age: Staff Sergeant Clayton Moss and the Capture of Sicily, The American Boys and the Liberation of Europe. My grandfather was largely cheerful and optimistic, with a bawdy candor that often seemed to forget his audience was still a child, not unlike that boy's letters to his own son decades later. My grandfather was also a steadfast patriot, and never doubted his country or the war it fought. *Maybe it's easier to feel like a hero when you're fighting Nazis.*

The last envelope in the pile was different. It was a Western Union telegram envelope, dated May 20, 1944. I knew what it was before I even opened it. Inside was a single creased quarter-sheet of thin beige paper imprinted with impersonal purple type. It was addressed to Mrs. Dorothy Moss. My grandmother.

The Secretary of War desires me to express his deep regret...

I imagined my grandmother receiving that telegram and dropping to her knees in shock and grief like Ruby Pierce described herself doing two decades later for a different husband lost to a different war. I imagined her telling her twelve-year old son why there would never be another letter from his father. In a sudden convulsion, I found myself bawling. I held that telegram announcing my grandfather's death in action in Italy, and I cried. I wept loudly and sloppily, like a toddler. When Dr. Collingwood told me about my father's death, I'd felt nothing. Now, I was a mess, grieving a man I never knew, a man I had known nothing about an hour before. *Dr. Midge would have a field day with this,* I thought.

All those letters from my father, all those years, and he never talked about his own father. Never once mentioned losing his dad when he was twelve. Never talked about how scared he must have been in Korea, knowing his father had been a wartime casualty less than ten years before. Maybe he thought I wouldn't understand. Maybe he shut it all out. Maybe whatever pain and grief he felt came out with the only therapist he ever relied on, a 1948 Remington Rand 5 Deluxe.

I set the telegram down on the pile of letters. The crying had stopped, but there was still a weight on my chest, one of those cartoon anvils sitting on my heart and my belly. *My grandfather fought in World War II. My father fought in Korea.*

Langdon Pierce in Vietnam, and May Pierce in Afghanistan. Three-quarters of a century, two families, four generations of American blood soaking forests and jungles and deserts around the world. Fighting for freedom, for empire, for profit, for security, fighting because they chose to or were compelled, but fighting all the same. Fighting was as foreign to me as the soil they bled on. I had never fought for anything in my life. Not baseball, not my first wife, not my writing.

My father had been a lover *and* a fighter. Not me. I was neither.

Moss

SECOND INTERLUDE

Excerpted from Wages of Empire

From the letters of Staff Sergeant Clayton Moss, 15th Infantry Regiment, 3rd Division, II Corps, to his son

August 18, 1943

You probably won't get this letter for who knows how long while the Army censors make sure I'm not slipping military secrets to an 11 year-old kid. Put down the sports pages, Isaiah my boy, the Yankees are going to win it all again even with DiMaggio taking batting practice in uniform to keep the rest of us Joes happy. What you want to see is on the front page. We took Sicily from the Axis like a class-A dame from a dead-hoofer at the USO. I won't bore you with details they'd just black out anyway, but I can say it's been hot work these past days and that's no lie. Patton pushed us in a sprint to plant the flag at Messina, and boy if we didn't beat Monty and his Brits there by a matter of hours. Old Blood and Guts, they call him, even if it's his guts and our blood. He's a fighting man, and he likes fighting men. There's certainly plenty of fighting to be had.

August 30, 1943

We've been cooling our heels here in Messina, but I'm spoiling for action. Send me and a few boys to Berlin and we'll black old Adolf's eye for him. I guess the road goes through Italy. That's fine. We can plant Old Glory in Mussolini's fat crack on the way. Messina is pleasant enough. I'm not sure if the locals see us as liberators or occupiers, but whether it's joy or fear, it amounts to the same. The women are happy to keep a Joe company either way, and the women are the only thing finer than the wine. If they leave us here too much longer, there will be more Italian-American babies here in a year's time than in Brooklyn. Your mom would tell me to hush and not say stuff like that to you, but you're what, almost twelve? I remember starting to notice the skirts around then, and I know kids are growing up faster than we did. I could swear some of the grunts in the Italian Army weren't any older than you. Tell you what, take my Winchester 70 and shoot some woodchucks in the yard. They dig up your mom's garden. And it's good practice in case the Nazis show up in Jersey. A man should know how to shoot.

October 20, 1943

Italy, though I can't say where. Fighting's pretty thick, which suits me fine. That's what war is, fighting. Fighting, and noise. You can't conceive the noise. It's like being inside the bell of Tommy Dorsey's trombone alongside all the other trombones in the world. The bullets sound the same when they hit the ground or a tree or a wall, a flat kind of dry slap. When they catch a leg or a chest it's a wetter sound, and then you get the sounds the fellows make when they get hit. Screams, sometimes, but often it's more of a grunt, like they're surprised they just got stung by one hell of a hornet. When the work is real hot, and the hornets are all around, men fall to your right and left, men you were just drinking with or pissing with or laughing with the day before. Gone in brief instants, here now then not, that sudden bullet out of nowhere coming for you like an unlucky card at the poker table. It's not the screams you remember if you live but the crying later, the quiet-like weeping in the night, grown men bawling like abandoned toddlers, bleeding in the mud, dying or wishing they were dying. It doesn't bother me so much. Each bullet that doesn't get me, whether it hits a tree or a man's leg, is one less Nazi bullet with my name on it.

January 17, 1944

Jimmy Cahill lost half his head to a bullet yesterday, not three feet away from me. Jimmy was probably my best friend in the Reg, a funny guy. The broads loved him, so he was a swell pal to have, you know what I mean? He was looking at me one minute and then the next his face was a melon split wide open. It was that fast. I figure if a bullet got Jimmy, odds are it'll be a while before one gets me. Fighting's been hotter than ever. No idea how many eyeties I've put down since I got into this business. Hundreds? Maybe. Better them than me. Boy, the blood gets up when the action gets hot. You know how you're leading off second and the batter laces one into the gap? You don't think, you just get your behind in gear and make heartbeat decisions about whether you can get home before that right fielder can get the ball back in. God, action is so much better than sitting around. FDR's cousin Teddy called it "the crowded hour". Well, old Ted, keep those hours coming. There's no bigger thrill in life than getting into the soup and then getting out again on the other side. You're a little nastier and a little faster and a little luckier than the other fellows and you see another day with another drink and another dame. If there's anything in the world goes down smoother than a willing woman after a tough fight, then I sure don't know what it is. Don't tell your mom, but I love it. Beats the living hell out of driving that old milk rig for Clover. Are you twelve yet? Find a girl, son. Even if you're just at the kissing-game stage, maybe a quick cop, there's nothing better. These guys here, they pray every night for the war to be over. Me, I pray that it never ends.

Moss

CHAPTER EIGHT

If there was a time when I felt closest to truly writing, it was when I was at Dartmouth. I arrived in Hanover armed with blue pens and a head full of words aching to find their way out, eighteen and still mostly unbruised by the unfairness of the world, eighteen and ripening on the vine, eighteen and a fool. There was possibility then, I can taste it on my tongue some mornings, when my conscious mind hasn't yet fully woken to the reality I've come to inhabit. In that instant between dream and day, before I open my eyes, I can sometimes forget that I'm a disappointment to that kid I used to be. The kid who was so sure he'd be a writer, the kid who actually believed the things our father wrote in those letters. The kid who didn't know all of his aspirations were on borrowed time, even then.

Some of my college memories have been lost, fogged by time or by choice (or by the occasional recreational indulgence in weed – I was an English Lit major, after all). There are classmates and even roommates who pass me in the halls of recollection and their faces blur, their names elide, their voices clumping into an unvarying and incomprehensible drone, like adults in the Peanuts cartoons. Some memories, though have only sharpened over the years, calcifying under the pressures of time and weight into sturdy fossilized versions of themselves, relics I can take out and inspect, wallowing or reveling in what they evoke. I can remember how it felt to read great books on the grass under the sun for pleasure and for purpose. I can remember the first time I met Kate Ingersoll, the first time we kissed, the first time we made love, even though that later turned to ashes. I can remember my first cigarette, and the explosive freedom I felt at all of it. *And writing*. Most of all, I can remember writing. Terrible, juvenile stuff, the most overwrought kind of florid prose, shallow characterizations, improbable meandering plots, but it gushed like a city fire hydrant in the hot summer. I wouldn't feel that way again until my father's cabin and my father's typewriter.

"I never went to college," he wrote me once during those years, "at least not as a student."

Oh, they invited me back, once my books found their way to the New York Times bestseller lists and their curricula. How they scrambled to find me honorary doctorates as pot-sweeteners for their commencement speaking invitations! Honorary doctorates. They accumulate like horse-show ribbons in a forgotten drawer. I read newspapers and walked streets, I listened as men spoke and watched as they lived, in Korea and Chicago and in the uglier corners of my mind. My writing teachers were my eyes and ears and my imagination, my final exams conducted by my publishers. No sheepskins for me except the fake ones, but then they're all fake, aren't they?

Still, if you're going to do it, make the most of it, I suppose. At least the women must be delicious. Are you still allowed to fuck women? Is that still a thing? Or is it hand-holding and chaperoned dances again? It's like the sixties never happened at all. Why did we bother having a sexual revolution if your anemic generation was just going to go back to wearing societal chastity belts? The papers make it sound like women are in charge now, in the board rooms and bedrooms both. Hell, maybe it's better that way. We certainly managed to make a damned hash of the world. Why not let them have a shot at it? I never minded a woman on top, myself.

One word of advice: don't let the academics look down their noses at you. If they knew how to write anything worth reading, they'd be writers, not academics. If any of them was worth a round tit, they'd be on that New York Times list instead of me.

Man, Isaiah Moss would have hated Sharyn Fitzgerald. I know I did, even though she was right. Dr. Fitzgerald was the first of the three women who would have such a pivotal impact on my life in those years. In the harsh, unvarnished vision of hindsight, I knew they were each right. It was me who was wrong, every time.

Dr. Fitzgerald was a Professor of Literature at Dartmouth, entitled to the capital letters because she was a full professor, with the invulnerability of tenure and several published works on literary analysis. They were antiseptic works of academia, arid treatises on form, but they were still books. My father would have considered them lesser works, pilot fish trailing the true sharks, scraping a safe existence from the leavings of their superiors, but to me they might as well have been hand-illustrated by monks in the Middle Ages. I had a profound and nearly pious awe of books as the apotheosis of human achievement, tangible and durable proof of our capacity for creation, their authors the wise ancients around our tribal fire, honored and celebrated. I wanted more than anything to be one of them, to hold my own books in my hands, to see others holding them, to see them stacked among the classics, beloved, immortal.

Second semester of my freshman year, I was registered for Dr. Fitzgerald's Introduction to Literary Theory class, and I couldn't wait. This was a published author, a heavy hitter in her field, a name the upperclassmen in our department talked about with reverence. There were fifty or sixty of us jammed into that old classroom in Sanborn Hall, seated on semi-circular risers in plastic swiveling chairs. At precisely the moment that first class period was scheduled to begin, Dr. Fitzgerald strode through one of the side doors with a book under one arm, a stack of papers under the other, and mounted the dais at the front of the room. The first thing you noticed was her explosion of bright-red hair, extending from her head in all directions like an Irish sunburst, unbrushed and unencumbered by convention. Little round glasses like Trotsky wore perched at the end of her long pale nose, behind which her face was a riot of dark freckles and glinting emerald eyes. She was wrapped in a various long and multicolored knit scarves over a large, shapeless cardigan, making her look like an oversized cat toy. There was a kinetic energy about her, an electricity as she sized us up, and I think most of us sat up a little straighter in our chairs.

The stack of papers was copies of the class syllabus, which she enlisted a nearby student to distribute. She then proceeded to read it aloud to us, slowly and pedantically, and as the minutes dragged on the vitality began to seep from the room, draining out of us into the tiered floor, a moment unseized. Questions were neither encouraged nor acknowledged. When she finished her narration, Dr. Fitzgerald looked up, surveying us from behind her Bolshevik eyewear.

"Dismissed until Thursday."

Without another word, she scooped up her book and was gone.

As the semester ground on, Introduction to Literary Theory became a dreary chore. I would wake up on Tuesday and Thursday mornings knowing it was on the day's schedule and wanting nothing more than to pull the covers over my head and go back to sleep. A colleague of mine at Arcadia years later once observed to me that schools would be wonderful places if not for all the students. She and Dr. Fitzgerald were on the same page. The class sessions were all pedantic lectures, usually variations on themes she had already beaten to a melancholy death in her books, and she seemed to regard students as a kind of disagreeable necessity, a hurdle to clear before she could get back to her real business of bloodlessly critiquing the work of other authors. Literature began to seem not a joyous expression of the human spirit but a kind of sterile mathematics.

While I was disappointed, something about Dr. Fitzgerald's icy reserve and joyless rigor made me crave her approval even more. I read her books and wrote my assignments with the grim determination of a private landing at Omaha Beach. When mid-terms came around in March, I filled that little light-blue composition book with confident and inspired prose, applying theory meticulously, citing credible sources, and marshaling cogent arguments. When they came back a week later, I opened mine and scanned the pages. There were no inked comments alongside my words, no circled phrases or underlined passages, no indication of where I'd done well or strayed from the path. On the very last page, in red marker, was the letter B. I was confused. I'd gotten similar grades before from other professors, but always with some indication of what I'd gotten wrong, or some suggestion of how I could improve. This was judgment without nuance, a Supreme Court decision without dicta. My confusion became irritation, and then anger. After class I decided to beard the lioness in her den and visit Dr. Fitzgerald in her office.

I don't remember much about the space she inhabited. It was an unmemorable faculty cubbyhole, full of books and papers and Sharyn Fitzgerald, hunched behind a computer like a spider in her web. When I entered, she seemed bothered by the intrusion.

"Yes, Mr..?"

"Kendall," I prompted. "Oscar Kendall."

"Very well." She removed her spectacles and rubbed them absently with the end of a scarf. "What can I do for you?"

"I wanted to ask about my mid-term."

"Dissatisfied, are we?"

"No, not with the grade. I mean, yeah, I guess I am. I honestly thought I'd done a good job. Can you tell me what's wrong with it."

I produced the blue book when she stretched out a hand for it. She replaced her glasses, riffled through the pages, and handed it back to me.

"It's a perfectly acceptable exam, Mr. Kendall." *Acceptable?*

"So why is it a B?" I asked. I wondered if she had even read it.

"Because undergraduate students cannot achieve an A in Literary Theory," she stated firmly, an impatient smugness to her voice. "An A is a perfect grasp of the subject matter. Undergraduates lack the capacity to grasp this subject perfectly. You should be satisfied with your B, Mr. Kendall. It is about the best you can hope for."

I was thunderstruck as I wandered out of her office and out into the March snows. Of course, she was right, in her arrogant and graceless fashion. Years later in graduate school, when I was tasked with teaching new undergrads literary theory, I found their grasp of the subject matter to always be imperfect. Not once did I have a freshman in my classroom who could fully wrap their brain around structuralism or formalism or any of the other self-important -isms academics have devised to classify and analyze literature as though it were science and not art. But isn't that the point of education? Not to evaluate but to elevate, to pass along knowledge and critical thinking ability, to nurture emerging intellects? Maybe I'm a sucker, but I gave out a lot of A's to flawed work in those days. I still do. Yeah, Dr. Fitzgerald was right, but she was wrong, too. Part of me wants to go back and express my gratitude. I didn't learn much about how to write from her, but I sure learned an awful lot about how not to teach. I'd tell her, but from what I've read in the glossy alumni magazines, she's since passed away. Probably throttled by an undergrad with an imperfect grasp.

~~~

The second woman at Dartmouth I can never forget was another faculty member, as different from Sharyn Fitzgerald as snow from fire. Senior year I was writing more intensively and more productively than ever before, churning out page after page for myself and for my instructors as our capstone creative project loomed. It was the final hurdle to clear for Literature majors before graduation, a twenty-page exercise in creative storytelling. We were each assigned an advisor to guide and evaluate us, and Threnody Jones was mine, an associate professor, not yet thirty but swiftly ascending the tenure ladder. Born to Ghanaian immigrants in London before moving to Boston for college, she wore her black hair braided long or swept up in a colorful kente-cloth headwrap, her accented English like something out of Monty Python.

She insisted that we call her Threnody and not Dr. Jones – "I'm a poet, not an archaeologist," she liked to declare – and so we called her Threnody. It seemed to fit with her restless energy and apparently limitless capacity for positive affirmation. Threnody always managed to find the value in a classroom comment or a written page, and we loved her for it. It was as though some ancient Nubian goddess of encouragement had wandered into our midst.

In the winter and spring of my senior year at Dartmouth, Threnody and I met weekly in a quiet side room at the Baker-Berry Library to discuss the writing samples I'd turned in to her the week before. I was telling the tale of an undertaker who fell in love with the corpses he prepared for open-coffin viewing, an exploration of traditional horror tropes and narrative beats in the style of Poe or King. She liked the idea. She liked the plot. She liked the character. But around Valentine's Day she expressed concern.

"I can't shake the nagging sense that I've read this before," she said, her sable eyes squinting in frustration.

"Like plagiarism?" I asked. That was a potential accusation scarier than anything I'd written.

"No, no," she replied. "Nothing like that. The style, the tempo, the word choice. It reminds me of someone I've read before." She chewed at her lower lip. "Never mind. It'll come to me."

In March she came to our meeting armed with her markups of my pages and a satisfied glow to her round face. She placed a campus flyer on the table between us, and from it my father's photocopied visage scowled up at us.

"Saw this on a bulletin board," she said. "Isaiah Moss is guest lecturing here next month! Isn't that exciting?"

"Exciting," I echoed dully.

"When I saw this, I was able to put my finger on it," she clapped her hands together in triumph. "I love solving a mystery – it's like finally getting that last piece of popcorn shell out from between your teeth! This is who your writing reminds me of! Isaiah Moss. The pages you've been showing me, it's like you're trying, consciously or not, to mimic his style. It won't do, Oscar. There's only one Isaiah Moss."

No shit, I thought, followed closely by *Thank God.*

I wanted to tell her. To explain that Isaiah Moss was my father. That my mimicry of his writing style was genetic and pathological and compulsive. That his was the shadow I chased, my own windmill to tilt at for all of my days. But I couldn't. I didn't want her understanding or her pity. I wanted her respect, and that was never going to happen on my own terms the moment I was his kid.

"Right," I said.

"You're trying to be him, and honestly not coming all that close. Only you can find your voice, Oscar, your own voice." She handed me that week's pages. "Can you do that?"

It was as though the entirety of the last four years had been a fraud, the free-flowing prose I'd authored a pale and laughable copy of the summit I'd never attain. *Maybe I should be just a cab driver after all.*

"So." Threnody seemed to sense that I had shut down, so she tried a different tack, holding up the flyer. "Do you think you'll go? I will. I know he's an old white guy, but I don't care. I loved *Holding Your Breath.*"

"No," I replied dully. "I can't make it."

The prospect of sitting anonymously in a full auditorium while my father bathed in the adoration of the crowd was more than I could stand. I knew I would never summon the courage to seek him out, to risk his brusque rejection or worse, to be unveiled as merely a satellite in his orbit, a lesser Jovian moon. I groaned inside, knowing Kate would want to go to. Like most students of literature, she had read a lot of Moss.

"I'll work on the rewrites," I stammered, and walked out.

I didn't go to the event. Kate did, with some friends, and later gushed about how amazing it was. I wanted to throw up. I suppose I should have been grateful she didn't go home with him.

~~~

Kate Ingersoll was the last of the three women. For a long time, I've lived with the sneaking terror that she was the love of my life, assigned to me mistakenly by whatever capricious divine bureaucracy handles that sort of thing. Kate and I were part of the same team project in one of our shared literature classes first semester. Funny and cute and smart, Kate had straight hair that I liked, a kind of long strawberry blonde waterfall that triggered latent Marcia Brady fantasies. A jeans-and-flannel girl in Chuck Taylors, a girl with no maintenance log in her glove box, she could shoot pool and drive a stick and loved to read almost as much as she loved to laugh. We studied together, watched movies together, went to lunch in the dining hall together. By Thanksgiving, she was my best friend at Dartmouth, and I thought that it made all the sense in the world to become lovers. I was young and still brainwashed by the saccharine stories Disney sold us, kissing a princess and true love and happily ever after.

When I first asked her out shortly before Christmas, she insisted it was a terrible idea and said no.

"You won't like it," she protested in the spring when I asked her out a second time. "You won't like me. And I want you to like me."

"I do like you," I'd replied, nineteen and stupid. "I think I love you."

"Isn't that what life is made of?" she sang to herself, lines from some goofy oldies song she knew but I didn't. She had a way of doing that – she grew up listening to AM radio with her mother, and she'd pull out odd lyrics and then look at me funny when I didn't catch the reference. When she told me "Billy, don't be a hero," I wondered for a week who the hell Billy was. Remember, this was in the dark ages before internet search engines and lyrics web sites.

"O, buddy," she said draping a frustratingly friendly arm across my shoulders, "I love you. You know that. I just don't *love* you."

I spent an entire year reading and writing and wondering what the hell that meant.

We eventually did start dating junior year, testament to my persistence more than her ardor. It was April when we kissed for the first time, drunk as skunks in the basement at some fraternity party. She'd been drinking hard cider and tasted like apples. Even now, I can't eat an apple without thinking of Kate. That Christmas I brought her home to meet my mother, and as we walked through the light snow in Connecticut, she told me she loved me. She lied.

Not long after graduation I proposed, during that terrifying interstitial time between college and real life when couples either break up or get married. Not long after, I told her about my father. It seemed like the sort of honesty you'd want between a man and his wife. Besides, I had invited him to the wedding, and she asked me, jokingly, if he was *the* Isaiah Moss. She'd met my mom of course, and I'd met her folks in their slope-side Vermont ski chalet during spring break, but when the subject of my father came up, I would just say we'd never met. It had the advantage of being almost entirely true. But I did tell her eventually, and she believed me. God, I can remember when we told each other things.

My father, of course, did not attend the wedding.

I am in receipt of an invitation from Mr. and Mrs. Ingersoll of Rutland, Vermont suggesting that I might come to the St John's Chapel in the town of the same name on August the 17th. I am, of course, otherwise engaged. No, that's not true. The truth is I choose not to come. It is a day for the child bride and child groom to command the spotlight, not some notorious interloper. I shall leave you to it. So young! Tell me, was there a bridal shower or a baby shower for your intended? My gifts to you both are enclosed. His and hers, if you will. I recommend separate accounts in anticipation of the eventual dissolution of your union.

The envelope included two one-thousand-dollar checks, one made out to each of us. My mother gave us a Kitchen-Aid mixer, cherry red like Kate wanted. My father gave us seed money for divorce attorneys.

They say men invented marriage as a way to ensure that the children they protect and provide for are their seed. That's probably true. Men are largely insecure creatures, possessive and jealous. Put a ring on a woman the way a dog pisses on a tree or a child licks the last cookie in the box. Mark your territory, growl at the wild wolves who skulk outside the ring of your fire. Mine. Warning. Mine. Such a waste of energy. Who gives a shit if the kid is yours? In all honesty I have no guarantees that I fathered you outside your mother's word. Of course, she lacks the wit to lie, so I probably did put you in her. You're certainly mine now in the sense that I've paid for you these many years. I don't believe in genetics any more than I believe in marriage anyway. I am not my father any more than you are me. To think otherwise is arrogance.

If men invented marriage, women invented love. They invented it to snare men, to entrap and mark us as their territory as well. I am disinterested in either. John Donne tried to tell us that no man is an island. Please. We are all islands. To think otherwise is to rely on others to provide the solace and the satisfaction we crave. There lies a dangerous path, boy. What someone can give you, they can withhold. Love, marriage, these are bargains doomed to disaster. Learn to depend on your own resources, to be content alone, and your heart will never break. You will happily drink at funerals for the rest of your days.

He was right, of course, and so was Kate. The marriage was a mistake. I didn't like being with her, not in the end. But then, women have always been impenetrable to me, and probably always will be. After we got married, the sex that had once been serviceably passionate melted steadily away into infrequent and indifferent. She never enjoyed it that I could tell, but then I don't know that any woman I've been with ever has. The deeper I get in my forties, the harder it becomes to ignore the possibility that maybe I'm just a lousy lover. You meet an asshole in the morning, you met an asshole. You meet assholes all day, maybe the asshole is you.

Kate Kendall turned out to be a shrewish and joyless version of Kate Ingersoll. The virtual entirety of her words to me were critique or assignment as we trudged through a series of apathetic arguments over things I've since forgotten and hardly mattered then. I was certainly no dream come true either, resentful and dissatisfied and mean. I was in graduate school for most of our wedded disharmony, working long hours teaching those sieve-minded undergraduates at Boston University and trudging through my dissertation, a miserable workmanlike paper on imagery in 19th century American fiction. I was unhappy with my life and grappling badly with the realization that I probably always would be. Kate and I rarely laughed anymore and never touched, chaste roommates in a cold bed who didn't really need each other to pay the rent. When the inevitable split came, I asked her when she had stopped loving me.

"I'm not sure I ever did love you," she replied. I didn't say anything. What do you say to that?

We divorced, after three years of listless marriage, largely without rancor and largely without regret. A breakup with paperwork, an exercise in sorting CDs followed by six months of vague uneasiness at being alone, and then nothing. I think I did love her, once, when the world was strawberry blonde hair and 70s lyrics and far horizons. We haven't spoken since the divorce. From what I can tell on social media, Kate Ingersoll has another last name now, and children. I hope she enjoyed making them.

CHAPTER NINE

My father was no stranger to brothels. In one extended Vanity Fair interview with his frequent comrade Gore Vidal back in the 70s, the two men went to Amsterdam and drank it dry of booze and hookers both. In loving detail, the article had described the professional Dutch sex workers, including some surprisingly sophomoric prose about nether lands in the Netherlands. The famous authors had incongruent appetites (Isaiah Moss almost slavishly hetero while Vidal mostly though not exclusively enjoyed sex with men) but both were unabashed patrons of prostitution. Isaiah Moss had few scruples about paying for sex. What he didn't like was paying for not-sex. That's why he hated strip clubs. "All-you-can't-eat buffets," he scathingly called them in one particularly memorable letter he sent me in my teens: "I know nothing manly about watching women undress to overloud music and then scrabble about on the floor for dollar bills and their dignity. Better to stay home and masturbate to a magazine, or else pay a premium and secure the full experience in private."

Not a living literary legend, I lacked the resources to arrange weeklong romps in the Low Countries, so I'd been to strip clubs, though never in the company of another woman. That was May's idea.

"It'll be fun," she said, with another of those shrugs I adored. I think she knew I adored them, and did them for me, her little teasing game. That made them better and worse all at once. "Let's drink and judge together."

So we drove south for two hours, to the north shore of Boston. In Lynn, the City of Sin, there was a gentlemen's establishment called The Pear. Nestled between a shuttered fried clam joint and a boot shop it lay in wait like some patient bear trap, a neon-framed ambush for the eagerly debauched. We parked at a nearby Motel 6, booked a room in anticipation of a late night, and walked the quarter mile to the joint, me on my feet and her on her prosthetics.

"I don't usually like walking very far on these legs," she said. "They make me feel like a pirate who didn't know when to quit."

"Do most pirates know when to quit?" May smiled, with her mouth enigmatically closed, the way she usually did. One morning over deck beers she'd told me more about waking up after the blast and the amputations, the confusion and denial, the sudden and grievous sense of loss, the ongoing and incomplete reconciliation with a new reality. How wrong it felt that her legs were gone. It just wasn't how the world was supposed to work. She had lived her life on her feet, and now they were simply no longer there, like waking up one morning to find there was no such thing as bread, or only twenty-four letters in the alphabet.

I opened the door and escorted May into the lobby of The Pear. It was surprisingly clean and almost classy, like the vestibule of a movie theater, with no suggestion that beyond the next door women took their clothes off for money. I paid the bored young man at the desk forty dollars – twenty bucks a head cover charge – and we were escorted into the club proper. It was dark, the way urban nightclubs are dark, and it took a few moments for our eyes to adjust. Thin lines of pink neon limned the ceiling, bodies crowding on all sides, music weighing down on everyone like a high-pressure weather front. Drum-driven rock music thrummed, low and visceral, resonating through the pelvis. A beautiful Puerto Rican woman was on stage, gyrating to something by Poison. Her lingerie was a shade of green that matched her lipstick and the streaks that ran through her caramel hair, glowing lurid under the club lights. A variety of men had staked their claims close to the stage with their wads of singles to dole out as tips to the performers. The writer in me was forced to observe them, to file them away as future characters. Frat dudes laughing and high fiving, drinking domestic beers. Dead-inside middle managers with loosened ties, reluctant to go home to sexless marriages and thankless children, drinking gin. Solitary broken regulars in sweatshirts, there for a glimpse of what they'd never get in the world, drinking fantasy. As far as I could tell, May was the only woman in there not dancing or waiting tables.

"Thank you Jade!" boomed the voice of the unseen MC as the dancer scooped up her green cash and her green underwear and scurried backstage. "Now give it up for…Sugar!"

This girl was black, with scarlet lips, corset, and thigh-high boots. The regulars hooted and clapped.

"Must be a fan favorite," May said.

Sugar did not dance so much as engage in an impressive rhythmic gymnastics routine involving the entire ten-foot height of the pole in the middle of the stage. Some rap song I didn't know pounded in time to her act. At one point her bra came off, clearly intentionally, though I never saw her hand work any clasp or strap.

"I can see why," I replied. A pretty waitress came to our table in a black leather skirt and crisp white button-down shirt, and we ordered our drinks. A Jim Beam on the rocks for me, a Grey Goose and tonic for May. I found our waitress sexier than the stage girls. A little mystery goes a long way.

"Do you think the servers are dancers on their night off?" I asked. "Or is it an entirely separate gig?"

"You could ask her." We didn't quite have to shout to hear each other, but almost.

"Nah." I liked the mystery. I could imagine our waitress as a brilliant sociologist finishing her doctoral dissertation and using this job as research. I could imagine her as a struggling poet or sculptor or singer. The reality would almost certainly be mundane and tawdry, so I kept the mystery.

We watched the women come and go on stage, all the while keeping that waitress busy. May was much faster than me, and yet it scarcely seemed to affect her. I had always thought that I could drink with the best of them, but May was in another class. May was a major league drinker.

"You drink a lot," I said.

"I could go toe to toe with your father," she replied, with only the suggestion of a slur, though her voice had grown huskier as the vodka tonics had chased each other down her throat. "If you had a father."

"If you had toes." I finished my own drink and swirled the melting ice in the bottom of the glass. "Why?"

"Why what?"

"Why do you drink so much?"

"It makes my legs stop."

"Stop what?"

"Itching. Trembling. Screaming. Begging to run." She swallowed a mouthful and cracked an ice cube in half with her teeth. "They're still there when I'm sober. Begging." The first hint of tears came to her eyes, and it made the hazel of her irises brighter, almost golden. "They only shut the fuck up when I'm hammered."

If May was a major league drinker, my father was in the Hall of Fame. The stories about the amount he drank and the names he drank with were beyond legendary, nearly mythical. Aside from his European exploits with Vidal and his pilgrimages to Hemingway in Havana, there was Beirut with Peter O'Toole, Vegas with Sinatra, and Palm Springs with Elizabeth Taylor ("lovely, but lazy in the sack" he'd told one interviewer). For all those glitzy escapades, he did his serious drinking alone, in the cabin, just him and James Beam and blank sheets of paper breathlessly awaiting his genius. *Was it their screaming, their begging, that Isaiah Moss was trying to quiet?*

We watched another couple of dancers ply their trade. The songs and the bodies were beginning to blend together, a harmonic convergence of music and flesh on a tide of booze. We'd apparently cycled through the club's roster; the emerald-tinted stripper who'd been dancing when we first came in was back on the stage, in a different flimsy green costume.

"Not much to judge tonight," I admitted.

"They're all pretty good," May agreed. The tears had never come, and the bulletproof façade was back up. "I guess we should have come on amateur night. Do you like her?"

"Jade?"

"Yeah. Do you want her?"

"I want them all. That's how this works." It was true. I'd been getting increasingly aroused during the evening's entertainments. It was getting to the part of the mystery when you wouldn't mind finding out whodunit.

"I mean for a lap dance." May moved her hips in her seat, biting a corner of her lower lip and fixing me with her eyes. The loose blouse she was wearing slipped a little off her shoulder, revealing a pale blue bra strap. Lights played across her face, red then yellow then darkness then bright white. The music pounded. It was achingly sexy, far sexier than the parade of commercial-grade nudity on the stage.

"I would love a lap dance." I returned her gaze. "But not from Jade."

"Sugar?" she asked. "Jinx? Charity?"

May was toying with me, grinding subtly as she rattled off the names of the dancers we'd seen. I didn't mind. It would be hard to find a more willing target of seduction than I was in that moment. I could taste her sharp-edged gritty flavor on my tongue, an urgent tang. God, I wanted her. And not in the way I'd wanted other women. Not to possess her or to use her for momentary gratification, but to bury myself in her, to abandon the now and the then and all the rest of time to be in her willing flesh. To drown, to forget, to achieve numb stupor. Some guys will tell you that sex and intimacy are about ecstasy, but they're wrong. When right, when skillfully performed between mutual seekers, it is the demolition of self. It is the ultimate shared anesthetic. And how I craved that oblivion. "The dream of the drop of water is to die in the sea," I was told once by a girl in college, Heidi something, a granola worshiper in loose cotton skirts who may or may not have been thoroughly stoned at the time. I'm sure she told me what trendy Eastern philosopher wrote it, but I may or may not have been a bit stoned myself.

Why the hell did she want to come here? I wondered. Was she just messing with me? Teasing me? Or maybe she had some other plan at work, maybe more than teasing. I was ready to find out.

"You want to get out of here?" I said, and I was a little surprised at how husky my voice was. Hoarse from competing with the loud, suddenly obnoxious music, I told myself. But I knew it was hunger. It must have shown in my eyes, because the gaze that May sent back was hungry too, intense and electric. She nodded.

I got up and dropped some paper money on the table, more than enough to cover our drinks and take care of the cute waitress. May stumbled a bit as she got up, whether from the quantities of vodka she'd swallowed or from the awkwardness where flesh met plastic and steel under her pant legs, I couldn't tell. She reached out to steady herself and grabbed my arm, just above the elbow. She leaned against me, not for balance but in that feline, fluid, seductive way a woman can when she wants to. We left the club and walked alongside Route 107, where red tail-lights still pulsed past with regularity at nearly two in the morning, steel and aluminum blood hurtling along one of Boston's primary arteries.

It wasn't long before we were in our hotel room back at the Motel 6. May clumsily yanked the drapes mostly shut and turned off all the lights except in the bathroom, closing that door so just a little illumination leaked out from the edges. She held a finger to her lips and pointed at the bed. Obediently, I sat. May took out her cell phone and squinted at it for a moment, evidently searching for something. In a moment I could hear the brassy opening bars of Joe Cocker's "You Can Leave Your Hat On" and I knew where this was headed. There are some songs out there that only have one purpose in life. "Life is a Highway" is for driving. "Stairway to Heaven" is for desperately seeking a partner before the last dance of the night in Junior High. "You Can Leave Your Hat On" is for a strip tease.

May was unbuttoning her dark green blouse, standing just a few inches beyond where my fingertips would reach if I were to stretch out my arm toward her. May threw her top at me and shimmied her shoulders in just her pale-blue bra and snug black jeans. I'd seen her in a bathing suit any number of times, but there was something indescribably erotic about seeing her like this. In the dim light, with that trite song, I might as well have been seventeen again, drunk on cheap wine coolers and watching a girl take her shirt off for the first time.

"Close your eyes," she said in a low growl, and I hurried to comply. Now all I had was Joe Cocker, getting to the part about standing on that chair. *Yeah, that's right.* Then I felt her weight on my lap, straddling me, her lips at my ear.

"Open them. If you want."

I did want. The heat of her was so close and so tangible, her bare shoulders and arms and stomach and thighs slick with perspiration. She had taken off her pants and her prosthetic legs, and one of her strong hands grasped the back of my neck while the other she ran up and down her own mostly nude body, writhing in place with the music. She still had her underwear on, a thong the same color as her bra. I hardly qualified as an expert on women, even less so on their diverse sexual habits, but my ex-wife had once told me that when a woman wore matching underwear it meant she expected to be seen in it. May had planned this, it wasn't just some spontaneous drunken escapade. I didn't know whether to feel complimented, used, aroused, or all three at once. The matter flew from my conscious mind as her quads squeezed either side of my pelvis with remarkable strength. A lithe and powerful tigress was astride me, her physique incredible as it throbbed against me, each muscle evident like the bas-relief of an ancient marble frieze. As the song ended, she found my ear again, her breathing hot and insistent.

"Did you like that?" she asked.

"Yes," I murmured. I wasn't sure I could manage much else.

She was kissing me then, wet and deep and not entirely accurate. Where so much of May was hard, her mouth was softer than I had imagined. Her tongue carried the thin metallic tang of vodka. Her hands were fumbling at the buttons of my shirt while she licked my neck, and I reached behind her to unhook her bra. In a single fluid motion, she swung her body around me and plunged onto the beige bedspread, pulling me down on top of her. I felt her body with my hands as we kissed, touching her angular shoulders, her defined abdomen, her stiff nipples.

"Now," she insisted.

I stood up, pulling off my clothes. I don't think I've ever been so erect in my life. I was the eighth wonder of the modern world down there, the Granite Obelisk of Oscar.

"Come on," she slurred, and I had climbed halfway onto the bed when I paused. It was the first time I had heard the booze on her voice that way. Looking down at May on the bed, in the shadows I couldn't see where her legs ended and didn't care that they did. I could see that her eyes wouldn't focus on me and her movements were clumsy, arms draped above her head in a floppy laziness. She was incredibly sexy. She was also hammered out of her mind.

I wrestled with the moment. If I'd been seventeen, it would have already been over. (To be honest, if I'd been seventeen it would have been over before Joe Cocker had gotten his first words out.) If we'd been together for years, I probably wouldn't have thought twice. But it felt wrong. Not morally wrong; we'd both been drinking, we were both adults. And she was willing, hell, she was practically begging. But all I could do was think back to that night on the dock, when she told me I needed a friend more than a lover. That evening in the barn at the farm, her hand on my chest, a gentle but firm rebuff. Oh, I still wanted her. *Jesus, I wanted her.*

But she didn't want me. Regardless of what she was saying now. Regardless of her matching underwear.

I knew my father wouldn't have hesitated for a moment. *I'm not Isaiah Moss.*

When I could feel myself going limp, I knew it was over. "No."

I wasn't sure at first if I had said it out loud or just in my own head. Her head swiveled to the side a bit and May peered at me with a single bleary eye, like a wary and confused bird. The eye squinted a bit.

"What?" she managed.

"No. I'm sorry. No. Not like this."

I took a slow step back, trying not to look at her, trying not to want her, trying not to wonder if I was a god-damned idiot. A cranberry-red paisley-patterned blanket had been folded on the bed before being knocked to the floor. I picked it up and draped it over her.

"The fuck?" she asked, pushing into a sitting position. I couldn't tell if it was a delayed continuation of her earlier "what" or its own distinct comment. The blanket pooled around her hips, just below her breasts. I was failing at not looking at her, so I picked up my jeans and stepped into them without bothering to put my underwear on. An hour ago, all I had wanted was to kiss May, to take her clothes off, to fuck her. Now all I wanted was to go back fifteen minutes and stop all of this from happening.

"You have got to be joking," May seethed. One of her hands was behind her, propping her up, the other held out in front of her in unsteady accusation. "You've been horny for me since we met and now I'm throwing myself at you and you're not interested?" This last word climbed the stairs of her vocal register two at a time, finishing in a high-pitched snarl of accusation and disbelief. She stared at me, mouth open, breathing just a little fast. The taillights of 107, a window and parking lot away, splashed across her face in an imprecise rhythm. A wet black line of mascara trailed from the corner of one eye, though from a tear or sweat, I couldn't tell.

"You're drunk, May," I said.

"Fuck you, Oscar." May seized the blanket and curled up in it like a child, turning away from me on the bed. "I'm always drunk."

I hoped her legs would shut up and let her sleep.

~~~

Streaming sunlight woke me up and I glanced at my watch – it was almost eight in the morning. A twinge in my back served notice that I'd slept on the cramped motel couch, and I gingerly unfolded myself from the Cirque du Soleil contortions I'd performed to manage it. At forty-three, things neither bent nor unbent the way they once did. May was still there, sleeping under the paisley blanket. I had half expected that she would have gone, calling a cab or stealing my car or strapping into her legs and walking back to New Hampshire. Nothing surprised me about May anymore. The only thing that surprised me was me. At forty-three, I hadn't thought I had any surprises left in me.

I slipped on my shoes and a shirt, grabbed my wallet and the motel keys, and headed for the Dunkin' Donuts we'd seen the night before on our return from the club. There is a law of nature in New England that any road with more than two lanes has to have a Dunkin's franchise every half-mile, and that morning I was glad of it. I had a slight headache from the booze and the noise at the club the night before, but I felt a strange sense of placid serenity, like beach sand before anyone has walked on it. Was this what it felt like to make the right choice for once? I wasn't at all sure how May would react this morning. I braced myself for the likelihood that she would be angry with me, and while I wasn't looking forward to that, I almost preferred it to how upset I thought she'd be if I hadn't stopped. It didn't really matter. I hadn't done it for her. I'd done it – or, more accurately, I *hadn't* done it – for me.

It was astonishing how many cigarette butts there were between the motel and the donut shop. I'd flicked my share out the car window during my own days chained to the leaf, never thinking about all the others who were doing the same. The butts clustered along the curb where the road shoulder met the sidewalk, a cancer salad garnished with empty nip bottles, a wet McDonald's bag, and one forlorn used condom. I wondered if it had been part of a cheap date

163

alongside the burgers from Ronnie Mac's Steakhouse. It had rained at some point during the morning, so the jetsam all stewed there together, soggy and fetid and forgotten. The rubber looked like some big white whale had washed up on a beach and been deflated, while the sodden butts looked like exactly what they were. I had given it up, but I knew why people still smoked. We are creatures of habit and ritual, and smoking is no different.

Don't smoke, Isaiah Moss had written to me when I was nine. *Unless you have to.* That was the extent of his Solomonic wisdom on the subject, which I promptly ignored in college and for years after.

There was a short line at the dingy Dunkin's, two men in construction vests and hard hats, a woman in a dark pantsuit, and a mom with a stroller. *America, writ small.* The hardhat guys were talking about a lead the Red Sawx had blown the night before, the pantsuit was typing furiously on her phone with both thumbs, and the mom was cooing to whatever was in the stroller. I listened to them all. I liked to listen. My father one wrote that ears are more important to writers than eyes or hands. When my turn came, I bought two medium coffees and a box of six donuts. Coffee can fix a lot. For the rest, you need donuts. I didn't know what May liked, so I got a mix. Glazed, chocolate, jelly, blueberry, Boston Cream, and a cruller.

When I got back to the motel room, May was awake. She was lying under the blanket on her back, her arms behind her head, staring up at the popcorn ceiling. Her eyes found me, and they smiled even while her mouth didn't. Clear eyes, sharp and piercing. How she wasn't hung over from the night before, I had no idea. May had the professional drinker's immunity to the morning after. She looked at the coffee and chuckled.

"A peace offering," I said.

"I'm not sure you're the one who needs to make peace," she replied, sitting up and clutching the blanket under her armpits with the ease practiced and inherent to women, like swaddling their wet hair in a towel, an ease foreign and bewildering to men. Her smile spread to her lips then, though it was rueful and a bit embarrassed. I shrugged, setting my tray and box down on the cheap nightstand.

"Then it's just coffee and donuts."

Something in my belly was fluttering, unsure and hopeful. May was a mess. Her short hair lay flat on one side and jutted up with sprightly indifference on the other. Her makeup from the night before had run or blotched, giving her the look of an extra from a low-budget zombie film. And yet…

"About last night…" May started, and I waved a hand.

"Don't," I said.

"Don't what?" Her eyes narrowed.

"Don't apologize."

"I wasn't going to apologize," she said. "I was going to say I used to be better at this."

"I've never been good at this."

"Yeah, it's not about you right now."

I sat on the couch and sipped at my coffee. May toyed with a loose thread on the cheap blanket, twisting the thin red line around her fingers.

"I thought boys were a distraction in high school," she said, looking down at her slow unraveling of a stretch of paisley, then back up at me. "The only thing I was serious about then was running. I made out once or twice with Danny up at the lake when his family came up from Philly for the summer, just kid stuff. I remember one time he stole some beers from his dad and tried to get me to drink them with him. Yeah, that wasn't going to happen. I wouldn't even kiss him with it on his breath. I told him you wouldn't pour piss in the gas tank of a hot rod. I was a hot shit back then, at least I thought I was. Christmas break senior year I gave Jimmy Archambeault a hand job in the back of his Mustang. He tried to put his hands down my pants and I damn near broke his nose. He must have been more honest about that than most teenage guys or else he spread a rumor that I was a cock-tease, because guys kind of gave me a wide berth the rest of the year."

"Coffee?" I offered. She just shook her head.

"At BC I dated one of the guys on the men's team. Harry Fast. That was his fucking name, I swear to God. Harry Fast. A miler. He was my first. I was twenty and figured I'd find out what all the fuss was about. Harry lived up to his name in bed more than he did on the track."

"Harry or Fast?" I asked.

"Both," she replied, making a bit of a grimace. "There were a couple of other guys, but no one worth talking about. I still had my goals, and getting pregnant—or worse, falling in love—just weren't in the picture. I had some fun in the Army, but there was no way I was getting hitched up to a soldier. I just couldn't picture spending more than a week or two with any of the guys I hooked up with, let alone the rest of my life, you know? When you run marathons, they have refreshment stations along the route, these tables with paper cups of water or Gatorade. You slow down for a second, grab one and drink it. It's great, but you don't stay there. You drink and you keep going. There'll be another one soon enough."

"You sound like my father."

I had to know.

"Was he ever...a drink?"

May looked at me as though a stray dog had wandered in off Route One and took a shit on the rug.

"I think he would have liked to be. And your dad robbed his share of cradles, for sure," she said. "But I had no interest in robbing a grave. So he contented himself with watching me swim. The way you do."

Even as I felt a tremendous weight lift off me, I felt guilty for having ever carried it in the first place. Having spoken it out loud, it seemed ludicrous, Isaiah Moss in his final decrepitude, seducing the sleek young mermaid from next door. It was only after a moment that I realized the implication of her last sentence. *I'm not content at all.* I stood up, set my Styrofoam cup down on the table, and pointed at the one I'd brought for May.

"Sure you don't want this?"

"I don't need coffee, Oscar. What I need is a drink."

She raised her arms, the blanket falling away from her naked body.

I stepped forward and put my arms around her, lifting her into an embrace. She wrapped both of her hands behind my head, and her lips found my neck, my ears, my mouth, then my ears again.

"Now," she whispered urgently, pulling me down to drown in the sea with her.

CHAPTER TEN

I had nightmares as a child. Monsters in my room, bo-geymen, the usual stuff. I lived as so many children did with the bedrock conviction that if my foot poked free of my blankets, it would become a handle for a vampire or were-wolf to haul me out of bed and away to their lair. My mother must have passed this intelligence along to Isaiah Moss in one of their rare communications, because one of his subse-quent letters contained some unorthodox advice on the mat-ter.

Never fear the dark. The worst things I've ever seen happened in the light of day. Children fear the dark because they fill it with the ghouls and bugbears of their fertile young imaginations, and so parents will leave a light on and gently instruct their progeny that no such creatures exist. This is bullshit. Without question, there are monsters under the bed, boy, monsters in your closet, lurking with sharpened claws and ravening maws to tear and worry at your flesh. That they are imaginary does not render them unreal. That they are the whole cloth inventions of your mind does not render them unreal. It makes them more real, because they are yours. You have made them. You could unmake them, I suppose, with a nightlight and a cup of warm milk. You could slay these fiends with the advancing grind of years, laughing with your ma-ture friends about the silly childhood fears you overcame. There are no monsters under the bed, you will tell your own small spawn in your smug self-satisfied stupidity. But you and I both know the monsters are still there. We are born to invent them; our minds are wondrous machines of creation. And terrors, both dark and light, are our specialty.

Never fear the dark. All there is in the dark is what we bring to it, the horrors we give shape to in the quiet moments of utter soli-tude while the tedious world sleeps with barren contentment. Em-brace your monsters. If you run from them, they will only chase you. Children who need a light on become adults who need Vali-um. Embrace your monsters, those lovely brutal expressions of

your mind. Yoke them to your service. Make them your muses.
They will never lie to you. Not like your parents.

My mother had gone the nightlight-and-warm milk
route, and eventually the nightmares receded, more from
my own aging than from her ministrations. But my father
was right – the monsters were still there. Werewolves and
goblins became anxiety and inadequacy, and still I ran. They
found me anyway. There were mornings when I'd open my
eyes before the sunrise and lay there in my sheets, feeling
the dark press on all sides, taunting, picking at unhealed
scars of doubt with insidious invisible tendrils. Sometimes
I'd fall back asleep, sometimes the only thing to do was get
up and banish the pursuers with mindless movement, or
maybe even with words on paper.

May had nightmares, too.

We began to share a bed that July, the creaky old
pinewood frame and double mattress in the cabin's only
bedroom. How many nights had my father lain there, alone
or not alone, stories churning in that fertile head? I tried not
to think about how many conquests he'd had there, body
and mind.

In the mornings, May would swim and I'd write or I'd lay
there and think about writing. Sometimes we'd go into town
for lunch at Thornell's Country Café or to poke around at
Mrs. Henneberry's antique shop. Mrs. Henneberry was a
grumpy old lady with long floral skirts and tan work boots,
stomping around her junk-filled shelves like she couldn't
wait for an excuse to kick a customer in the ass. She made
me think of my first-grade teacher, which made me root for
the customers. May liked it there. Children don't go to antique shops.

In the afternoons and evenings we'd drink and look at
the water, or drink and talk. I liked the talking more than the
drinking. May had stories about my father, things he'd told
her that he'd never put in his letters to me. It didn't matter
whether they were true or whether he was just trying to
charm and seduce her with tall tales. I liked hearing them.

One time, when we were especially deep in our cups, she repeated a story Isaiah Moss had told her about one week in the cold spring of 1951 when his unit was ordered to remove the civilians from a village called No Song Ri in southern North Korea ahead of the planned US bombing of a nearby bridge. Not all of the civilians complied. A clutch of old men, and mothers with small children, mistrustful of men in United States Army gear and their South Korean allies, refused to abandon their homes.

"If they didn't move, if we couldn't get them to move, we bombed that bridge anyway," my father had told May. "We'd have been better off just shooting them in the head and moving on."

May told me about how hollow his eyes had gotten then, and how one of his hands fluttered. How almost seventy years later he could still see the faces of the villagers he couldn't convince to save themselves, how their blood still clung to his hands.

"Look around the lake sometime," May told me after that story. "Look how many of these places have flags flying. You don't see one here, do you? No Song Ri."

As the sky grew dark those evenings, we'd eat something and maybe fool around a bit in bed, though we hadn't made love since the motel. The sex was secondary to the intimacy, something I'd never experienced before and had never really considered. Eventually, May would fall asleep. Sometimes I'd fall with her. Sometimes I'd try to write some more.

The night was when the monsters came.

She never screamed or thrashed or woke in a cold sweat. Nothing so cinematic. She would twitch, murmuring unintelligible words of anguish, the sheets a damp tangle from her struggle against unseen, dreamt-of adversaries. In the morning when I awoke, her side of my father's lumpy bed would be abandoned. Wraiths sought her in the night, black and ruthless, flaying with memories that would never forgive. Her only escape was the dawn, which was just an escape into a different nightmare.

It was around ten o'clock in the morning on the last Thursday in July when I decided I couldn't stand it anymore.

"May," I said, and she looked at me. Her eyes were red-rimmed, exhausted, vacant. The Furies were whipping with extra vigor that morning, savage and intent on their punishing business.

"Oscar," she murmured, barely audible.

"Let me help."

"No one can help." Her carriage had always been erect in her chair, a soldier at attention even seated. Now she was slumped. It was a posture of defeat that broke the heart I didn't even know I had.

"I never..." I paused, trying to think of the right way to phrase what I was thinking, wanting to help. I wanted to tell her I was there for her, that even though I'd never been there for anyone in my life, I was there for her. I swallowed, and just said it. "I never thought I would be with someone like you." Before the words had finished forming in my mouth, I knew it was a mistake. Have you ever seen highlight films of a pitcher who grooves a fastball to a home run hitter and never turns to watch the ball after it leaves the bat? He just hangs his head. He knows he fucked up. May went suddenly rigid, her mouth almost disappearing into a twisted scowl of withering disappointment, her eyes glinting with dangerous hurt.

"Make sure to claim 'fucking a cripple' as a charitable deduction on your next tax return." She spun her chair around and set her hands to the wheels to leave.

"May, wait!" I yelled, and I grabbed one of the handles of her chair. She twisted, and the entire apparatus fell to the floor, spilling her across the carpet with a cry more of rage than pain.

"Never touch my chair!" she howled. Her face had gone red and splotchy, and she laboriously heaved herself back toward the toppled wheelchair with her arms, dragging what remained of her legs behind her. I reached out a hand to help, and she smacked it aside, hard. This was different than the spill on the track. That had been us together, in harness against an unfair world. This was me as just one more idiot incapable of understanding her pain, incapable of helping.

I was profoundly frustrated. Maybe my father had been right about women. No attachments, like some drunken sex Jedi, stumbling about the galaxy from woman to woman with never a concern to spare about the human detritus in his wake. Except I did care about May, and I didn't want to hurt her. And yet I did. I always did. I thought briefly of Juliet, and then of Kate. I knew I'd screwed up with my ex-wife, hell, that it ever happened at all had been me screwing up. She'd told me it was a bad idea, just as Frances Root had warned me about May, just as May herself had tried to push me away. But like a fool, I wouldn't listen. Kate had told me she never loved me, and I wondered if I never loved her either, only the idea of her. I wondered if I was doing the same thing now, if I was unfairly trying to make May Pierce into what I wanted and needed her to be, just as I'd done to Kate Ingersoll.

I stood there, watching as May clawed back up into her chair, absurdly reflecting on my absurd first marriage. With a sudden hot explosion in my belly, I rejected my own ludicrous premise. What I felt for May was real, I knew it, and I wasn't going to let it go.

"You think I care about your damn legs?" It burst out of me without thought and without warning. I'd been fully prepared not to say anything again, to let the first woman I'd cared about in almost twenty years drift away like Kate had, but something in me rebelled at the prospect. "I mean, first of all, I'm a boob guy."

A snort came from May as she spun and hoisted herself into the seat of her chair. If I thought making her laugh was going to help, I was wrong. But I didn't know what else to do.

"You're a jerk," she said, not without affection, but not with very much of it. "And not even a very interesting one. God, I thought at least you'd be interesting."

"You mean like my father?" I asked. It was like invoking a demon without a pentagram.

"Your father wasn't a jerk," May replied. "He was an asshole. The most egotistical asshole I've ever met, and I was in the Army." She paused. "The guy fought in Korea and hunted with Hemingway and got drunk with Mayor Daley. So yeah, interesting. Even if half the stories he told me were probably bullshit. What do you care? He's dead and you're not." She cocked her head slightly to one side. "Are you?"

Maybe.

Every instinct in my body screamed *fuck it*. This was too much work. Too hard. I hated hard. Hard was my high school baseball coach suggesting an extra hour each day of batting practice learning to hit a curve. Hard was the prospect of sending my manuscripts to agents and getting rejected. Hard was figuring out what Kate wanted and giving it to her. I didn't do hard. I once heard an Olympic running coach on TV say the difference between gold and last place in the 100m final was a quarter of a second. And a quarter of a second was found in tenths and hundredths and thousandths of a second every day over a lifetime of hard, over and over and over. Who does that? Who has the patience and discipline to repeatedly inflict that kind of pain on themselves, no matter how lofty the goal? Not me. I had my father's passion for the written word, and maybe even some tithe of his talent, but none of his ambition. When it came to effort, I was my mother's son. And yet, as I looked at May, I knew being with her would entail that kind of work. Was I capable of that?

I knelt down next to her and took one of her hands in mine.

"Maybe," I said. "But then, how alive are you?" I didn't know where it came from. It was a ballsy thing to say, and ballsy wasn't where I usually found myself. Before she could respond, before she could get pissed off or push back, I kept talking. "We're both broken people, May. Misfit toys." I forced myself to look in her eyes, in her bewitching, skeptical hazel eyes, instead of at the wall or her lap or my shoes. "Want to find an island together?"

The slap came sudden and hard, against my ear and cheek.

"You think I give a shit about your father? About you?"

May had raised herself up on her chair with her arms, quivering and hovering inches above the vinyl of her seat pad. My face tingled in a way that told me the pain would come later.

"I don't give a shit about myself. I wake up every day with regret that the fucking sun came up again. So don't sell me your island. I don't want it."

"Well, I do!" I was bellowing. I'd never bellowed before. It wasn't something that came naturally to me. But I suddenly found myself fighting for something I believed in, something I wanted desperately, ardently, perhaps for the first time.

Instead of arguing with me she sighed, ragged and long, sinking back into the cushion of her chair with exhausted resignation. Her face was blank as she looked at me in numb defeat.

"You don't get it," she said. "It's the helicopters."

"What helicopters? There aren't any helicopters here."

"That's the worst part," she replied. "When we could hear the rotors, that meant there was air cover. That meant we were safe. We could sleep. When it was quiet, that meant we were alone. When it was quiet, that's when the attacks would come. That's when you would make sure you were ready to run."

"Look at me," she sobbed, eyes red, pulling at her hair. "Look at my fucking legs!" she screamed, pounding at her thighs with tight-balled fists. "I can't run!"

The monsters never stop coming for her, I realized.

"If you can't run, I'll push you. I'll carry you. I'm here."

"I can't." The sudden fire had gone out of May, the brief spasm of her rage spent. Her face was wet, her sharp cheeks tear-streaked. "I can't..."

"You can."

I was on my knees, my hands clinging to the armrests of her chair. Blood pounded in my ears, my scalp, every capillary of my flesh. I couldn't let go.

"You have to," I begged. This was what Frances had tried to tell me, about how deep May's pain went, but in that moment I didn't care about what some lesbian farmer thought or what my father might have written. I cared about May.

"I'm here," I repeated.

She sagged, her head drooping, and tears fell thick and slow the way a toddler cries.

"Just hold me, Oscar," she said. And I did, as hard as I've ever held anything in my life.

~~~

On the last evening of July, May went over to see her grandmother for a while. I sat at the typewriter, looking out over the lake as the light faded, wrestling with the words that came hard, if at all. Time passed, and stars began to prick against the ceiling of the world. I toyed with a glass of bourbon that tasted wrong. It was hot, my shirt sticking against my sweaty back, the bottoms of my thighs clammy and damp where they met the chair. It was half-past eleven when May came through the door on her prosthetics. Like me, she hadn't really had anything to drink that night. It was just too damn hot.

"Oscar," she said, and I turned to face her. Whether it was how the half-light of the dimly-lit cabin fell across the sharp symmetry of her face, or the way she said my name with possessive familiarity, my pulse quickened. She walked into the room, slowly, looking at me the whole time with those fathomless hazel eyes, like an unworried cat. When she was close enough, she put a hand on my shoulder.

I think I'm in love with her.

"Yeah?" I'd been annoyed with how badly the writing was going that night, but my irritation melted away like so much butter in that heat. I smiled and put one of my hands on hers. She took it, stroking it a little with her thumb, looking at it as though it were her first time seeing one.

"Let's go out on the lake," she said, quietly, as though someone might hear, as though we were high school sweethearts trying to sneak away to make out. "We can take the canoe."

There was a fiberglass Old Town canoe over behind the Pierce place, under the porch. The hull was forest green and badly scratched, the once-white interior stained, and the screwed-in wooden seats were splintering, but it was a tough old craft. I think it was at least as old as I was. We'd been out in it a few times that summer, just wandering the coves and crannies of Franklin Lake, but never at night. I was tired, and about to say no, when May asked again.

"Please," she said.

"All right."

The Pierce cottage was built on a cinder-block foundation like so many of its mid-19th century peers, pine over concrete, whatever materials were at hand. The canoe was still there under the porch, snuggled between forgotten fragments of deck furniture and a small pile of cinder blocks stored up for eventual repair work. At the moment they served as low-rent housing for sleeping chipmunks and watchful spiders. We pulled the canoe across the short slope to the water, the fiberglass whispering softly against clover and thistle. With the choking heat and my own fatigue it felt heavier than usual. The white birches guarding the shore were just shadows, hints in the darkness, standing in their silent disinterest as we approached. There was a small break in the stone wall lining the shore, maybe five feet wide, where the water lapped in to form a little beach. That was where we thrust the canoe into the shallows and shoved off, the wooden blades of the paddles grinding wetly in the sand.

Once we were floating free May took off her artificial legs, slowly, almost lovingly, and laid them carefully in the center of the boat. The clunk of the metal against the fiberglass was amplified, its echo carrying the way noises will on the water, especially at night. It was dark, but not as dark as the night we'd talked on the dock behind the Pierce cottage. The stars were out, and so was the moon, though it kept ducking behind some high invisible clouds, casting a pattern of spidery shadows on the surface of the water. It was a little cooler out here, and that was nice after the intense heat of the day. May was wearing a dust-beige t-shirt with the word ARMY in bold black across the chest and black shorts, and I found her impossibly lovely as she glowed in the starlight. We paddled quietly, almost gingerly, as though our strokes might break glass instead of water. There was a kind of spell cast over us both, a paralysis and pleasure that I never wanted to end. Somewhere, another cove over, a loon wailed. Eerie as they could be, they were beautiful once you got used to them. *The death of childhood made music.*

Rather than hug the shoreline, May guided the Old Town out past the mouth of the cove and into the wider main body of the lake. Franklin Lake was shaped almost like a cross, with a long central stretch unevenly bisected by two smaller arms. Under other circumstances I might have been a bit nervous about traversing the middle of the lake at midnight in a small boat with no lights; larger traffic routinely came out of nowhere, tearing ass down that long middle expanse. But I wasn't worried. I knew nothing bad would happen. May was with me, and the night that cloaked us was part of the magic that would keep us safe.

Read your Sherwood Anderson, my father had written to me years and years before. *He understood that small lives are still lives, full of agonies and miseries and loves and triumphs, and no less full because of the smallness. I never met Anderson, but Hemingway did, and I met Hemingway. Ernest told me no writer ever understood human nature better than Sherwood Anderson. Of course, we were drinking rum and he said all sorts of things, but I agree with him. "It may be life is only worthwhile at moments,"* Anderson wrote. "Perhaps that is all we ought to expect." Find your moments, boy. String them together like pearls.*

"Come here," May said, huskily. I shuffled toward her, crouched low, my hands on either gunwale for balance, every heartbeat a perfect pearl. Our faces came together and she kissed me with a tenderness I'd never felt before, from her or anyone. It seemed to last forever, a moment that was all the pearls at once, the entire string on its own. When we broke apart, May's face was damp with tears.

God, I love her so much.

"Sit," she said, and I did. It was quiet then, for long moments. Even the loons were at peace.

"I can't do this anymore. I can't do it to you, or to me. It hurts too much."

"What?" I asked, cold with a sudden fear. What was she talking about? "I don't..."

"Hush," she said, and I did. "This...this fantasy. I wanted to believe...but it hurts, Oscar. No, not my legs, though they do and that hurt never goes away. No, the hurt is here," she pointed to her gut, and to her head, and finally her heart. Her tears had stopped. "It's everywhere. And all the therapy and medication and booze and sex in the world isn't going to stop it. I've tried. The hurt just gets worse."

"No." I almost couldn't get the word out. My tongue was lead, my mouth wool. "No, please, May, let me help. We can..."

"We can what? Live happily every after?" She half-smiled then, almost sweetly, with just a hint of her teeth glinting in the starlight. "Maybe that can happen for you. But not for us. Not for me."

There was something in her hands then, something thin and gray and flexible. *Clothesline?* She was looping it around her waist, one, two, three times before tying it off. I tried to move, to reach out and seize hold of her, but that paralysis that had been so warm and beautiful had calcified into an unwelcome straitjacket. I begged my arms, my hands, my legs to move, but nothing would work. It was as though I were watching something that had already happened, something I couldn't change if I wanted to. And I wanted to. Sweet heaven, I wanted to.

"I love you," I croaked.

"I know you think you do," she said, her voice firm but not unkind. "But you don't, not really. I don't love you. I wish I could. But love takes a kind of hope, and I don't have any left." She looked up at the stars, around at the trees tiny against the far shores, and blew out a long, low, shuddering breath. Reaching underneath her seat, she picked up something square and heavy with her sculpted arms. It was half of a cinder block with a length of line tied to one end.

"I..." but whatever else May Pierce had to say remained unsaid. With a quick, decisive swivel she slid over the side of the canoe into the black water.

"May!" My scream echoed across the quiet midnight, the lake a perfect black mirror except for the splash. Whatever had been holding me let me go, and I sprung in a crouch to the other end of the canoe. I could see the white, ghostly outline of May Pierce, her face looking up at me in a pallid rictus of farewell and apology, receding swiftly into the murky darkness below. In his cabin my father had a wavy-lined topographic map of the lake on the wall, like what fishermen use to figure out where to go. I'd stared at it one night in a drunken haze, imagining what glaciers or springs or watery demigods had carved out its contours. In the middle, where we were, Franklin Lake was more than a hundred and thirty feet deep.

Without another thought I was in the water myself, water that even at the end of July, even with as hot a summer as I could remember, was still an icy shock. It didn't matter that I had never learned to swim. All I could see was her face, her shoulders, her neck with that birdcage tattoo, plunging down into the middle of the lake. I pointed myself down, orienting on the pale, dwindling smudge beneath me, and kicked. My shoes came off, and I thrashed at the water with my arms. Cold and indigo it closed around me as I dove with desperate panic, carving my way into depths that did not welcome me. Bubbles streamed from ahead of me, May's final breath, a fading trail to where I couldn't follow her. I made it twenty feet down before the pressure against my ears and my own terror forced me back up, up, up, in search of air. My head burst free of the surface, I gulped greedily for air, and then forced myself down again. Except the ghost was gone. There were no bubbles, nothing to follow, nothing to chase. Nothing.

I surfaced again, finding the canoe and clutching it with my cold hands. I screamed over and over again, for May, for help, for God, for anyone. *She'll come back up any minute now,* I thought wildly. *She's such a strong swimmer.* I saw her as I first saw her, a golden knife against the waters, a mermaid, a miracle. *She tied a lousy knot. The line will break. It's a joke, a prank. Please. Please. Oh, God, please.*

I don't know how long I was there, screaming, begging, praying. At some point green and red lights appeared and came closer, a voice coming over the radio asking me questions I tried to answer while my teeth chattered so hard I thought I'd tear my tongue to ribbons. It was the Marine Patrol, the guys who motor around checking for fishing licenses and drunken boaters. I told them what happened. The two guys, young guys, fit guys, looked at each other.

"How long?" they asked me.

They didn't even dive. They wrapped me in blankets and towed the canoe back to the cabin. I was too tired, too scared even to sob. I sat there in those coarse government-issue blankets, numb from cold and terror and sober realization.

May was gone.

Moss

CHAPTER ELEVEN

The Fish and Game guys must have called ahead, because when they brought me inside the cottage a town cop was already there. Ruby was standing by the window, her lined face an unreadable mask, looking out at the lake. In the rising dawn, the water shone with an unfair red-gold beauty. The skinny kid with the badge and red-blond mustache was a part-time officer, accustomed to drunk snowmobilers and unlicensed deer hunters. He seemed nearly as stunned as I was by what happened. There hadn't been a drowning in Franklin Lake for more than thirty years, he told us. Even with that peach fuzz on his lip he looked almost young enough to be one of my students at Arcadia. As I answered his questions and he looked over my body for signs of a struggle, it vaguely dawned on me that I was being considered a potential suspect. When the State Police Forensics specialist showed up a few hours later, I answered the same questions in the same sequence. I sat there, wrapped in that same blanket, almost grateful for the shock deadening all of my senses. When they started discussing sending divers to retrieve May's body, Ruby had heard enough.

"No thank you," she said, in her grating, suffer-no-fools voice. "I think we're through here. I gave you fellows the note she left. This boy had nothing to do with it, and she doesn't want you poking around down there looking for her. She wants to be let be, and there'll be hell to pay if she's not."

The forensic guy looked at the town cop, a conversation as brief as it was silent.

"Yes, ma'am," the mustache said. "My initial report will indicate no foul play." He turned to me. "Sir, you're free to go."

I doubted I would ever be free again.

"Understand," said the forensics guy, "if the body is found, we may re-open our investigation."

"It won't be," Ruby declared with stony finality. "I taught May her knots myself, when she was a girl."

I've often thought about the young cop since then, just a kid trying to do his job and maybe even help people once in a while. Isaiah Moss had sent me a letter when the streets of Baltimore, an hour's drive from my apartment in Maryland, were a battleground between protesters and police.

Cops aren't superheroes. They're not Batman or Spider-Man or even Dick Tracy. They're not pencil-and-ink archetypes of brawn and courage. They're flesh, they're clay, no inherently nobler than you or I except that they wear a badge and walk a beat between the bad guys and us. I knew cops in Chicago, when I was a cub reporter. I worked with them and drank with them, in uniform and out. Just men. Were some of them dirty? On the take? More than a few. But they had kids who needed shoes and braces and school-books, and city pay was a joke. When the gangs reached out with a little extra here and there, a few steaks or some folded greenbacks to take a nap or some junk to pass along, who would be the wiser? Mrs. Smith got a new coat and the rackets ran their numbers. Most of the guys were decent. But a shit system will turn a decent man to shit faster than a politician's promise after election day.

I read the papers. I'm not a fool. The shit system is getting shittier. And when it starts to go bad, you have a choice. You can do what you're told, or you can stand up against what's wrong. Boy, wrong will win every goddamn time. It always has. Wrong is undefeated. I don't blame people for throwing bricks. I'd be pissed too if I were them. I also don't blame the guys who put a uniform on every day. The hell of it is that they both believe they're the ones standing up when they're both just doing what they're told.

I'm glad I'm too damn old to care anymore.

I didn't care anymore, either.

By mid-August Franklin Lake had basked in what passed for summer sun in New Hampshire for weeks, shedding enough of its customary frigidity for the casual swimmer or vacationing families with their little ones, but I was uninterested. I would never put a damn toe in that lake again, or any lake for that matter. I was uninterested in a lot of things. I hadn't written anything in days, my father's typewriter enthroned in mute, metallic reproach by the window. Taunting, teasing. I kept plying myself with bourbon, trying to tame my grief, trying to summon and seduce my muse, to escape into words, but they wouldn't come. I kept drinking anyway, hopes of liberating creativity eroding into numb self-medication.

I never drink to get drunk, Isaiah Moss wrote to me when I turned eighteen. I didn't know then if he was unaware that the drinking age in most states had been raised to twenty-one since his youth, if he assumed I'd ignore that rule like everyone else, or if he simply didn't care. *I drink to avoid sobriety, that torturous, unnatural state. Grapes are natural. Wheat, corn, potatoes. Hell, rice is natural, though sake is tepid pisswater. Rye is the most natural of all. Resistant to cold, thriving in poor soils. When rye pollinates wheat, the resulting hybrid is stronger. Rye is the Nietzschean* Übermensch *of the cereals, the swinging dick of the grain fraternity. And bourbon, its purest expression.*

The purest expression of the swinging dick of the grain fraternity wasn't helping, but I kept drinking it anyway. The bourbon went down like holy water but it didn't help. No matter how much I swallowed, it didn't help. It didn't unleash or absolve me. It just made me drunk. May was still gone. And the words were gone. James Beam sat there on the crappy coffee table and mocked me too, brown and superior, with the same silent mirth as the typewriter. I could feel the waves of derision and disdain cascading from them in smug concert, a tangible miasma of contempt.

Your father was a better writer.

Better drinker.

Better lover.

Better man.

Your father would have saved her.

I tried to grab the whiskey bottle by its neck but only succeeded in knocking it over.

"Fuck you," I slurred, and grabbed it with both hands.

I threw it at the Remington with remarkable accuracy. The bottle shattered on contact, sending glass and bourbon in all directions. The vandalism felt good. Why should anything be whole or unbroken? What gave it the right? "Writing is an act of creative destruction," my father famously said.

"Fuck you too." Whether that was directed at my father or his typewriter I wasn't sure, but the two were synonymous in my foggy mind at the moment. I lurched up from the couch, nearly fell, and steadied myself against the coffee table. The room wasn't spinning, but I could tell it wouldn't need much of a nudge to start. I'd had too much to drink lots of times in my life, many of them this summer, but there was a blackness to this drunk, a vicious, savage dark. All the grief I felt for May, the grief I hadn't felt for my father, rose in my gorge like bile or vomit and poured out of me in an anguished cry. Grief, and guilt. *Why couldn't you save her?* In the canoe, in the cabin, in the past? *Afraid,* I thought, my brain capable of framing only single words through the thickening haze of liquor and loss. *Weak. Flaccid.* Enraged by my own inadequacy, I plowed across the floor of the cabin, leaning from side to side as it rolled like the deck of a ship at sea, aware of yet unbothered by the shards of glass digging into my bare feet. I fixed my hatred on the typewriter. The bottle had gotten what it deserved, but the ravening maw inside me demanded more punishment, more vengeance, so now that arrogant metal bastard was going to pay.

I seized the Remington with both hands. This wasn't vandalism, this was sacrilege, apostasy, rejection of the gospel of Saint Isaiah. Droplets of amber liquid beaded on the white keys and stained the blank paper in the roller. It was going to get wetter than that - it was going into the lake for a long, dark nap. Under the water with all those beer bottles. With May. I could see her lifeless face, pale and cold, her long thin fingers wrapped around brown bottles full only of tears. Shrieking, I lifted the typewriter off its table. Christ, it was heavy. The wood beneath where it had sat was darker than the surrounding surface by several shades. Who knows how long it had been since it had been moved? Years? Decades? My father had been here since the 1970s, making his immortal art. And everything he gave the world, the world loved.

Except me.

Nobody loved me.

Not my father, who put it in writing.

Not my wife, who told me as much when we split.

Not May, who chose death over me.

Screaming with all the breath in my lungs, bellowing in bourbon-fueled agony, I lurched away with the typewriter in my arms. *Crack!* My knee made sudden, solid contact with the corner of the coffee table and the jolt of pain made me drop the Remington. It struck like solitary thunder, splitting the wooden flooring where it landed. I fell alongside it, cursing and clutching at my knee. I imagined my father laughing from whatever corner of purgatory housed him and found myself laughing too, though nothing on God's spinning Earth was funny, even as the tears came. What a fucking waste it all had been, my entire joke of a life.

It was then I thought of the Colt .45 in my father's bedroom.

I can end it. I can stop the waste. I can be with May.

Except she didn't want me in this life. Why would she want me in the next?

I lay there, my face inches from the upside-down typewriter, more broken than it was. The only apparent damage was that one of the letter keys had popped free from its housing and rolled a foot or so away. I could see it there in the middle of the floor, a white ceramic island in a sea of knotty pine.

Reaching out, I picked up the wayward key, fumbling it a little with my booze-clumsy fingers. On one side was a small round indentation where it married up with the lever of the related type-bar that struck the platen and tattooed the paper in between, moving one letter from the mind of the writer to the eyes of the world. I turned it over. The other side, the letter side, was a perfectly round white disk inlaid with a slightly oblong black "O". *O for Oscar, Oscar like the Grouch.* I stared at it for a moment, bullying my drunken mind to grope for the geometric beauty of the oval and circle, the stark contrast between the ivory and the ebony. Maybe it wasn't an O, but a zero. *Zero like nothing. Like me.* It was cool in my hand, a steely token, a talisman. I had broken off a piece of my father.

Except it didn't matter. He was in ashes and May was in the lake and I was alone and empty.

My eyes closed, and I fell asleep.

~~~

"Enough, Oscar."

I opened one eye, and then the other. It was like lifting manhole covers with my eyelids.

Ruby Pierce was there, in my father's cabin.

"You're going to kill yourself," she said.

"So what if I do?" I croaked. "What do you care?"

"I don't," she replied with a rusty sigh. She was standing over me with her hands on her swaybacked old hips, like a mare rode hard and ready for stabling but not quite yet the glue factory. "But Isaiah would have."

I laughed, a kind of hollow cackle.

"He never gave a shit about me."

"Have it your way." Ruby righted the coffee table and set to straightening up the mess I'd made of the cabin. She was dressed just as she had been the day we'd met, in baggy shorts and baggy sweatshirt and baggy skin, tortoiseshell hornrims, her flesh leathery Yankee armor. Yet she seemed bigger somehow. I forced myself into a sitting position. The world swam a little, my head hurt a lot, and my knee throbbed. Everything hurt. And May was still at the bottom of the lake.

"What do you want?" I asked. Sun was spilling in through all the windows, bathing me in light I didn't want.

"I want May back," she said, taking a broom from the hall closet with the practiced familiarity of someone who had done it before more than once. "I want your father back. And for the love of Christ I want Lang back. Can you give me what I want?"

"Of course not." I succumbed to the inexorable comfort of gravity and laid back down, closing my eyes.

"No, no one can." She swept. No one had swept since I got there in June, so there was plenty to sweep.

"A thousand suns will stream on thee," she quoted in a quiet but firm voice, accompanied by the rhythmic whisking of the broom. "A thousand moons will quiver. But not by thee my steps shall be, for ever and ever."

"Tennyson," I said, folding my arms over my face. "At least you didn't go with ''Tis better to have loved and lost...'"

"Tennyson got me through when Lang died," she replied. "Tennyson, and Poe. Men who knew grief, real grief. There's grief, and there's sulking. Around as long as I have, I know the difference. You're a grown man, ain't you? You should too."

"Hey."

"Hey, nothing. May died two years ago in Afghanistan. Her body came home, most of it, but her spirit never did. You loved a shadow of a woman, boy. An Indian summer. I did, too. But that wasn't my granddaughter. It was only what lingered after war killed her just like it did my Lang. She was no damsel in distress for you to rescue. The only one who could save May gave up on her a long time ago."

"Who was that? Who gave up on her?"

Ruby's look made me feel like an idiot.

"May."

"Yup. She planned this, you know. She's been closing doors all summer."

The pictures and medals and trophies in her room. Her last lap. Doors closed.

"May," I muttered. Her name sounded both strange and familiar in my mouth, like a lyric to a song I'd once known complete but now could only hum. I lay there, wanting desperately for my head to stop hurting, wanting desperately not to think about May. So I thought about Ruby. I thought about how she lost her husband as a newlywed, how she lost their daughter to drugs, how she was now saying goodbye to the girl she helped raise and her late-life love in the same summer. And while I laid there on the filthy floor, hung over, she was sweeping. I wondered how many times she had swept here, had cooked meals for my father, had been the rock in his winter. I wondered how long their domestic arrangement had gone on. I tried to remember when he had first mentioned her in his letters to me, but his words swam in my head.

"How long?" I asked in a croak.

"Long enough," she replied. I don't know if she thought I was asking about how long I'd been on the floor, or how long she and my father had been together. I guess her answer was sufficient for both questions.

"Did you read it?"

Ruby stopped sweeping. She leaned on the long plastic handle of her broom, next to a growing pile of dust, sand, and dead ants. She clearly knew I was talking about his manuscript, about *The Last Sane Man*.

"Nope. Didn't have to. I wrote it."

I sat up again, heedless of the jolting agony in my temples, and then willed myself to stand, unsteadily, climbing a rickety ladder I didn't fully trust. I stared down at Ruby. She didn't seem so big anymore.

"What?" I asked.

"The cancer was eating him again," she said. A bead of sweat was running down her cheek. Or maybe a tear. "It did that, off and on, these last years. It didn't get him, though. His heart and his head conked out first. That's how I found him, right there by where you had your tantrum these last few days. Came over to fix dinner and he was slumped on that typewriter. Arms around it, like some kind of embrace. Thought he was asleep at first, or else passed out drunk. What was odd was that he was sitting there. He never sat there anymore. Arthritis, you know, in his wrists and fingers." She held up one of her own chicken-foot hands, scaly and meatless, in case I didn't follow. "He could barely light a match or pour a glass. Not that he didn't keep trying. Isaiah was a man for his appetites, no doubt. No, it had been near on a year since he last touched that typewriter with anything more than nostalgia."

"A year? So are you saying you wrote this manuscript on his typewriter while he wasn't looking?"

"Don't be stupid, boy. He was looking every day. He told me what to write, and I typed it for him. He could still talk, and think, and tell his stories. Hovered over me like an expectant father."

It fucking figures, I thought. *Isaiah Moss spent his last months in a prolonged threesome with the two loves of his life.* I shook my head. And then I laughed.

"You're shitting me."

"Nope." Ruby was using the dustpan to scoop up her swept pile. I looked at her, trying to see her through the eyes of a man staring down the end of his days, the eyes of a man who had known more firm young flesh than any horny soul could ask for rather than my own eyes, eyes that had never found anything they looked for. As the leaves fell from the branches of his aging limbs, Isaiah Moss had found not a conquest but an equal. A mind that understood him. A partner. *A friend.*

"I did lie to you earlier this summer, though," she said.

"About the dog?"

"The dog...?" She seemed to remember her bullshit story about the spaniel and the stone, and she let out with one of her brief dry cackles. "No, about Isaiah." She dumped the dividends of her sweeping into the trash barrel next to the refrigerator, and put the broom and the dustpan back in the little closet. Turning back to face me, hands on hips, she fixed me with that beady little stare of hers. "About Isaiah and you."

"Isaiah and me."

"That day when you first parked up yonder. The first time we met. I told you he never mentioned you. That I'd never heard of you. Lord above, boy, I never heard the end of you."

"What?"

"The Isaiah Moss you knew and the one I knew were different animals. Oh, he was a horse's ass. Mulish stubborn, and carrying his share of hurt plus some. He could never have written what he did otherwise. But he didn't keep you away to hurt you, or because he didn't care about you. For one thing, he didn't want you to have to fight your way out of his shadow. It's a long shadow, and heavy. He wanted you to be your own man, not his knock-off." Ruby's sigh rattled deep in her chest, and she looked gray and haggard, older than her years. "Whatever he had to give, he gave you in those letters he wrote. And he was broken, boy. Keeping you at arm's length was for you, not for him. He wasn't being a bastard keeping you away. He'd have been a bastard to let you in."

That sounded stupidly familiar.

"You know your Blake," she said, putting a hand on my arm. It made me think of my mother, of the care and love and worry of her touch. Ruby's skin was warm and tissue-paper thin. I could almost feel the steady thrum of her worn pulse. *Mothers never stop being mothers,* I realized. Not when their sons are grown men, and not when their daughters are long in the ground.

"Of course."

"Father, father, where are you going," she quoted, looking out the window at the lake, but I knew she was seeing some page in her crowded, memorized library, summoned by her nimble memory. "O do not walk so fast. Speak father, speak to your little boy. Or else I shall be lost..." Ruby Pierce wiped a tear away from her sandpaper cheek and shook her head at me, admonition and impatience and substitute love. The grip of her claw on my arm tightened.

"The night was dark, no father was there," I replied, the first line of the second stanza of William Blake's poem, but I couldn't get out any more. Ruby waved her free hand in the air while the other still clung to my arm.

"Blake's parents understood and indulged him," she said. "He also had no children, so what the holy hell did he know? These poets, these writers. We put them on pedestals and grovel as though their pronouncements are gospel. As though gospel itself is gospel." She sighed, and for the first time since dinner in her cabin a thousand years before, I remembered that she was an old woman. "You might not believe me, Oscar, but your father loved you, at least as much as a man like him could love at all. He tried so hard to speak to you in the only way he knew how."

"I...I don't know what to say."

"You never do," Ruby responded, and the age fell from her like a dropped shawl, the mask of the stern harridan hitched back on. "You never know what to say or to do. What about your father's manuscript?"

"You mean my father's and yours." She shook her head and made a disgusted sound.

"Oh, it's his. All of it. You think I'd dare to add any of my words to his?"

"I think you'd dare a lot of things." My head was throbbing, and all I wanted to do was drink some water and lie down. "I haven't decided."

"I think you have," she replied.

Is that right? I had the beginnings of a glimmer of an idea, but the debate was still an ongoing one within me. Everything you ever wanted in exchange for just your integrity is a bargain that better men than me have taken many times, and gladly. I wanted to claim *The Last Sane Man* as my own, to explode on the literary scene as a new genius, to append my name to the roster of greatness my father headed. Why would the old bastard have left me the cabin and its contents if that hadn't been his plan? His parting gift to me? I wanted Kate and Professor Fitzgerald and Cooper Clay to see my name in all the bookstores, to think that I'd done something important. Sure, Professor Fitzgerald was dead and who knew if Cooper Clay could even read, but Kate would see it. Even if it was a lie, only I would know. Well, only me and Ruby, and she wouldn't tell anyone, she'd just sit up here in her cottage and be disappointed in me. I wasn't all that concerned about her opinion of me. I was more concerned about my own.

"While you stand there with your tongue in your hands and your head up your ass, I have something for you."

"Is it...is it May's note?" I didn't know if I was ready for that.

"Nope. Whatever she had to say to you, she said to you. That was for me. *This* is for you."

She handed me a small book bound with faded green leather. The front cover was deeply scarred and the back was missing entirely. Several of the pages looked singed on the edges. The slim volume landed in my hands with the weight of a bank safe.

"What is this?" I asked.

"Lang's war diary," she said. "His story, in his words. Tell it with the others, in yours. And maybe someday you'll have a pedestal of your own. Not one you inherited or stole, but one you built yourself."

~~~

The next day, I mounted a testicle.

Alongside the shoreline behind my father's cabin rested an enormous boulder the size of a dump truck. A glacial erratic left behind thousands of years before, it was roughly rectangular at its base, but the surface sloped sharply upward from about five feet at one end to nearly twenty feet where it jutted out into the water. It was an impressive piece of geology, looking for all the world like an animated mandrill was going to present a lion cub up there. My father had written to me about it once, though I hadn't realized it at the time. Perhaps ten years before he had battled testicular cancer, and he had written in his signature detail about the experience. He had survived it, of course – what ambitiously dividing cells could thrive in that whiskey-and-smoke saturated habitat? – though he'd ended up having one testicle removed.

193

"One stone for the Scrotum," he'd written me, "but such a stone!"

Here it was, nestled among blueberry bushes laden with overripe fruit. I smiled as I rested a hand on it. *The Great Testicle.* I scrambled onto it and clambered on all fours up to the top. There was sort of a platform up there, a flattened disc about six feet in diameter. A thin blanket of rock-cap moss covered much of the gray stone like an emerald toupee, thriving furtively in the shade of the maples and shaggy hickories overhead. At the modest summit the sun prevailed, and the moss grew thin and sparse. I scraped some of it aside to unearth the naked rock and sat down, dangling my legs over the edge, looking out over the lake.

Granite.

My ass felt at home.

I unslung my backpack and rested it next to me. From its depths I procured a cigarette and lighter, a thermos, a blank yellow legal pad, and a blue flair pen. A shitty Paper Mate blue Flair pen, the kind I used to correct spelling and grammar and syntax on my students' papers and to jot my encouragement or bewilderment in the margins. My Arcadia students half-jokingly called it The One Pen to Rule Them All, the omniscient and omnipotent pen that would pass judgment on their juvenile efforts. Here, it would be a cheap thunderbolt in the hands of an imperfect Zeus, an implement not for evaluation but ejaculation. I lit the cigarette, and smoked it slowly, savoring the familiar ashy tang, watching lazily as my smoke drifted out over the still water. It was hot out, would get hotter still, and I welcomed it. When that first cigarette was finished, I lit another. In a fairy tale, the thermos would have been full of coffee. But we've established that this isn't a fairy tale, and there was bourbon in there. Not the old man's Jim Beam, though.

After Ruby's visit, I had restored the Remington to its mighty perch and sat behind it for hours, staring vacant and barren out at the lake. I found the "O" key in a pocket but didn't even try to reattach it. Instead, I pried another key off with a butter knife hoping that would make me feel better. I was wrong. I tried returning to the manuscript I'd been working on all summer, but the illusions had lost their power. It wasn't terrible, but it wasn't anything I was proud of. Every line made me think of what Threnody Jones had tried to tell me at Dartmouth twenty years before. It was passable, B-grade Isaiah Moss fan fiction. I burned it in the fireplace.

The next day I went into town, the little hamlet of Pendleton, where there was a liquor store. This was New Hampshire, where the state enjoyed a monopoly on spiritous beverages, and you were never more than half an hour from retail access to the sauce. I bought Jack Daniel's, a couple of the big bottles. Traditional black label. I also went into a rustic place called Hooker's down the street, a curious little general store that offered up milk, beer, bait, and smokes. A mountain of a woman named Rhonda sold me some Camels and peanut M&Ms. Neither of us smiled.

I smiled now, just a little, atop the Great Testicle, smoldering Camel dangling from my mouth. I wasn't over it. I'd never be over it. Every time I closed my eyes I saw May's face looking up at me as her body sank under the water. Every night as I fell asleep I felt the cold slap of that same water against my skin as I dove uselessly after her, screaming her name above the surface and below until my own lungs threatened to fill. Whenever I laid down I felt the hard smooth fiberglass of the canoe against my back in my exhaustion and panic and despair.

The grief was still there, and the guilt with it, but the edge had dulled, if only just. It didn't hurt to breathe any more, to live any more. Sometimes when I closed my eyes the sight of her face would start out white and sinking and hopeless and then it would be alive, thrown back beneath the early-summer sun as she sat basking on the dock. I knew there would come a day when I could recall May with joy, but I also knew the sadness would always be there too. *She was never yours to save*, Ruby had told me that morning when she nudged me back from the precipice of self-indulgent despair. That was a bitter pill to swallow. I was raised on the mythology of damsel-saving, raised to emulate Lancelot or

Zorro or Han Solo. I was weaned on stories where I was a hero. *The* hero. There was no space in my world view for the agency of the damsel, for the possibility that her story existed independently of mine, saving or not a narrative that depended on her and not on me. I realized I never asked her what her tattoo meant, if it even meant anything at all. And now I'd never get the chance.

The water rippled and danced below me, kinetic and random. A leaf, red-brown and dying, floated and danced in the rhythmic ebb. Even in the rising heat of the day it was a first whisper of the autumn that was not so far off, and I knew our time together was short.

As it so often did, the inspiration had come to me while I was shaving. You know how the moment the barber sweeps the cloak over your arms or someone hands you a sleeping baby, your nose starts itching? It's like that. Those few minutes with my wet hands and lathered face, pen and paper as good as uninvented, are when my mischievous mind unfailingly seems to find its its muse. Staring at myself in the mirror, listening to my own brain shout words and flash pictures at me, rushing the blade across my chin in a race against myself. This time, the images and coalescing prose survived the rasping and rinsing and were still with me now. I reached back into my backpack, sliding out the thin diary Ruby had given me and thumbing through its brittle pages. There were letters in there too I'd brought from my father's secret cache, and the letters he'd written himself, etched in my memory. Halfway through my third cigarette, that great and terrible blue pen began to move across the paper.

Scratch, scratch, scratch.

I read, I remembered, and I wrote. My words and their words, warp and weft on the loom, Lang's and mine, Clayton's and mine, Isaiah's and mine. May's and mine, distilling that fresh pain into prose. I was writing, telling and growing their tales, filling in the gaps with invention, weaving it all together into a larger narrative. I wasn't chasing the shade of my father's greatness, but plumbing my own truth, a shared truth.

Scratch, scratch, scratch.

Creation, Isaiah Moss wrote to me years before, I don't remember when, *is not bleeding at the typewriter, not the agony of midwifery. It is joy, sometimes painful joy, but joy nonetheless. It is God on all six of his workdays, it is the rendering of spirit onto paper, the uncloaking of personal truth for all who dare open the cover. It is nudity, the self laid bare, exhibitionism and conceit and hope. Writing is the celebration of a total lack of artifice, words as the fierce immediacy of confession. Go into the booth, son. Spill your guts. Tell your story. And then do it again, always begging for hollow forgiveness and the fleeting attention of the reader. The reader is dust on the water, vapor in the wind. The reader is nothing. Their approval? Their scorn? Empty, soulless. The confession is what matters, not the forgiveness.*

And so I wrote. I wrote and smoked and confessed.

~~~

As readily as the words came to me on that rock, they had come less frequently and with less volume from my father as he aged. It was as though his emotional prostate had swollen with time, impeding the flow of sodden sage advice that had been such a strong stream in his prime. It may also have been that it was less fun to dispense counsel to a grown man armored with his own ideas than to a guileless child. In any event, the letters after college slowed to an intermittent trickle. Always letters though, always. Isaiah Moss was not a man for phone calls, and certainly not for emails. He once wrote a thousand words to me on the evils of computers, including the laughably neurotic claim that the quiet hum of electronic circuits interrupted the firing of the synapses in his brain.

And yet, I saw precious little erosion in his facilities. The decades of bourbon and nicotine preserved him, like one of the jar-brains in *Young Frankenstein,* A.B. Normal until the end. The letters were all typewritten, masking any creeping frailty which shaky handwriting might otherwise betray. The last one was brief, less than a single page, coming just a couple of months before his death. I thought about what Ruby had told me, and I wondered if she had typed this for him too. *Probably.* That cagey old broad had known more than she'd let on, from the moment we met.

I am unfraid.

I have never been a man for professions or protestations of faith. Though the end draws ever nearer, so near I can smell the keen edge on the dread reaper's scythe, I am unafraid. Don't drag your ass, Thanatos. I am curious, indeed, I am anxious. No church has answers for what lies next. I remain unconvinced that anything lies next. This life is likely all there is. And this life has yielded itself up to me like a wet maiden, open-mouthed and open-legged, eager. And yet a man can have too much. As a young man you sit at table, ravenous, ready for the feast to come. Headfirst you dive in, to all the courses and all the wines and all the delicacies that follow. It is a lovely fiction, the feast. But there comes a time when you are replete, when you've devoured what was set before you, with seconds and even thirds. When all you really want is to leave your chair and lie down. To sleep, maybe forever.

There are some who don't live that way. Who pick at their food, who grumble about the choices set before them. There's an insanity to that, an insanity I don't understand. Who doesn't want to consume and engulf all of the banquet? Who nibbles? I am the last sane man, boy. The last. I wish I had faith that you would relieve me of that burden, that you had it in you to seize the world and take it all. But you're your mother's boy, not mine. You were made for gentler pursuits, for picking at your food.

I should have had a son.

I would have been concerned about him, but it seemed the vague ramblings of an old man rather than my world-weary father's final goodbye. Even his vague insults were tired, and failed to hurt. I was busy with school, with softball, with Juliet's old quilt and new breasts. Isaiah Moss was immortal. There would be another letter.

Moss

But there wasn't.
At least, not yet.

CHAPTER TWELVE

August was over, and it was time to leave.

It was still summer-hot, boats on the water and swimmers in it. Labor Day Weekend with its Budweiser and paper-plate cookouts was still yet to come, and as long as that act in defiance of seasonal change lay ahead, it was still summer. There was still time to laugh and splash and pretend school and work and snow were imaginary figments. Summer was when the lake was alive, at least on top. Below, on the lake bottom, there was death. Dead bottles, dead bottlecaps, dead soldiers. And somewhere out there, May. Hot as it was, I shivered. Hot as it was, it was cold where she slept.

The prospect of ever going back to Franklin Lake was too ghoulish to contemplate, so I sold the cabin. I tried to give it to Ruby, but she didn't want it. New Hampshire lakefront real estate is already wildly over-valued, but given its notoriety as the place Isaiah Moss wrote and died it ended up going for just north of two million bucks. I tried to split the proceeds with Ruby, but she didn't want that either. *Damn Yankee.* So I kept half of the money for myself. My head wanted to keep it all, but my heart wouldn't allow it. It didn't feel right. The cabin had been my father's legacy, never mine. I considered donating the other half to a foundation advocating for the as-yet-unbuilt national memorial to veterans of the wars in Iraq and Afghanistan, but then decided I would try to think about the living instead of the dead. I gave the money in May's memory to the Walter Reed Society to help wounded veterans. *Maybe I'm charitable after all.* I thought about what Ruby had said, about building my own pedestal. *Well past time to start.*

I didn't take much with me from the cabin. The typed manuscript of *The Last Sane Man*, his typewriter, his cufflinks. A couple of his high-end French-cuff shirts that fit better than I expected. And my grandfather's letters, of course. The morning I left, I fulfilled his wishes, scattering his ashes along the shoreline behind his cabin. Then I hurled his pistol as far out into the water as I could. It was a throw I think would have made Coach Watkins proud, even if it was still short of May's beer bottles. *Hey, if I'd had a better arm, I'd have played third base.* It was still warm but overcast and getting more so. The surface of the lake was a smooth gray slate, unmarred by boat traffic, the dark clouds threatening enough to keep even reckless out-of-towners off the water. When the rain came it would break the heat, and this time it wouldn't come back until next year. Even with Labor Day still in the future, the warmest days were gone. I thought about the Wheeler kids. Maybe Ruby would let them run and jump off the dock next summer. Maybe years from now, they'd tell their own kids tall tales about the scary crippled lady from next door. Maybe one of them might even try writing it down. We all live somewhere, even if we're just bit players in someone else's story.

A pair of loons drifted past in the cove, always bigger than you think they'll be. I'd always heard that loons mate for life, but when I said that to Ruby one day she just laughed.

"Loons find new mates each season," she said. "Just like people."

It started to rain, and the loons vanished, diving under the water to feed. As I got into my car I could hear their cry echo around the lake. I decided my father was full of shit. There was nothing musical about it.

I haven't seen Ruby since. As for Frances Root, I think she knew what was coming. I think Frances said goodbye to May that morning in front of the farmhouse. I decided Frances was full of shit, too. We never have had that third beer.

It rained the rest of the day. I hate the rain.

~~~

I stopped to see my mom on my way south. She lived in a little house in Stamford, not far from the city. We had bounced around when I was a kid, from town to town along the Connecticut shore as she found different jobs. Waiting tables in Mystic, answering phones in East Lyme, stocking shelves at the Bradlees in New London. New town, new school, new friends. After a while I stopped bothering with the new friends part. What was the point of getting emotionally invested in someone you were going to have to say goodbye to before you needed a new shoe size? It would be like getting an old dog from the pound. Remember the three straight years winning the kid writing contests? That was in three different elementary schools. That's why it was in the paper. By high school I pretty much just played baseball and went to class. I did the going to class part with sufficient success that I got into Dartmouth. When I lived in the same apartment in Hanover all four years, it was the first time in my life I had the same address four birthdays in a row.

My mom was restless, never comfortable, always looking for something. I used to think she was looking for what she thought she had found with my father, but she wasn't going to find that in these seaside Connecticut towns, serving lobster rolls to heavyset New Jersey tourists or reading meters at the beach parking lot. It wasn't even like she needed to work all the hours she did. My father was sending checks, big enough to pay the rent and keep us fed. So what was she looking for? She never finished high school, running away from her family in rural Nebraska at seventeen, running away from ranches and cornfields to chase movie stardom. It was 1974 and she was going to be the next Patty Duke or Karen Black, a sexy middle-class brunette who could pose for some pictures and then become America's cinematic sweetheart, or at least maybe a second-tier Bond girl, the one who dies in the first twenty minutes.

The problem was that she was a lousy actress. I asked her about it once, when I was eleven or twelve and starting to ask questions about things like that. She smiled and told me she struggled some remembering lines, but mainly she had trouble pretending to be someone else. Peggy Kendall simply lacked the imagination. She did a stretch as a model, some of it wholesome and some of it less so. I've never seen the pictures, but I've never gone looking for them either; no boy needs to see his mother in – or out – of fishnets and garter belts. Then came the seedy movies, not quite porn but within shouting distance. In 1976 she met Isaiah Moss at a party and nine months later she met me in a Los Angeles hospital room. As far as I can tell, she never modeled, acted, or saw my father again after that brief inspection in my earliest days. She simply gave up on all of it without a fight. Like I said, I was my mother's son.

She greeted me at the door, still beautiful. At sixty-three her raven hair had given entirely over to the silver of steel wool, and her figure had long since left fishnets and garter belts behind. It didn't matter. She was my mother and she was beautiful. Without a word, she drew me into a long, fierce hug. Hugs were her answer to most things, and it was hard not to love that about her. As women age, they seem to erode or expand, becoming either shriveled twigs or the shape and consistency of a marshmallow, and my mother was the latter. Being hugged by her was like sinking into the pillow top of an extra-soft mattress, sinking back into childhood, into the infinite simplicity of her love. I was three with a skinned knee, eight with a bully at school, fourteen with my first broken heart.

Whatever knots I'd tied to hold myself together came undone and my mother held me while I cried. I don't know how long I was there in her arms while she stroked my hair and rocked slowly back and forth. We hadn't spoken since that early phone call at the cabin. She had no idea about May or manuscripts or any of the rest of it. She didn't ask any questions or demand any answers. All she needed to know was that her son was hurting, and her hugs were what she had to give. I don't know how long we stood there together in her doorway. There are moments, even now, that I wish I was there still.

Eventually we broke apart and she led me into the kitchen. I sat at a little table while she made tea.

"Do you want to talk about it?" she asked while busying herself with kettle and mugs.

"I'm afraid I'll start crying again," I said.

"Then I'll hug you again."

I looked around. It was the kitchen of an aging but not yet old single woman, clean countertops and flower magnets on the fridge, the window over the sink bordered by buff-and-blue curtains with a neatly-pleated valance. On one wall was a framed newspaper article with a picture of a ten-year old me in black and white, the white yellowing with time. My mother saw me looking at it and smiled.

"That was when you won the third young author award," she said. The pride in her voice was as fresh as if it had been three days ago instead of thirty-three years.

All I could see were spiderwebs of cracks in the glass that weren't there.

"Her name was May Pierce," I said, and told her everything.

It took three cups of tea and some coffee cake my mom had on hand for me to get it all out. I didn't cry again as I talked about the cabin, about his book, about my book, about May and Frances and Ruby. I didn't tell her everything about Ruby. I never in my life intentionally hurt my mother; it would be like kicking a puppy. She sat there and listened, holding my hand hard while I described what happened the night with the canoe. After I told her about Isaiah's ashes that morning, it was quiet for several long minutes.

"He used to call me," she said, with a sad little half-smile. "Once a year or so. We'd talk about you. He wanted to know how you were getting on with your studies, with your baseball. He never asked much about me."

"I'm sorry," I squeezed her hand, which was still holding mine. "I know he was the love of your life."

My mother looked at me with a tilt of her head.

"Oh Oscar," she said. "The only love of my life was you."

The flush of red shame crept up my neck and into my cheeks as the proverbial ton of bricks cascaded down on my head. *Fool,* I cursed at myself.

I have a vivid memory of the day I first realized I was smarter than my mother. I was six, and we were on the couch in one of our living rooms in one of our apartments. I can't remember which town we were in, but I can remember that we were reading a book. She read to me every night after dinner and before bed, Golden Books or Doctor Seuss or Goodnight Moon, things like that. That night I brought her a Paddington Bear book I had found in the school library. I had read the first chapter on the bus and was tickled by the adventures of the furry little guy from Darkest Peru. I couldn't wait to share it with my mom.

"Oh, honey," she said on the couch, setting Paddington aside. "Not tonight. How about Richard Scarry? You love Busytown."

She had blushed that night, as I was doing now, because she was embarrassed and ashamed, as I was now. That book, that silly kids' book, scared her. Not the way some parents might feel scared moving from picture books to chapter books, scared because their son or daughter was growing up faster than they were prepared to accept. My mother was scared because the book was too hard for her, and that night we both knew it. That was her shame. Mine was that it mattered to me so much, and for so long. For nearly forty years, my regard for my mother was predicated on her literacy, her intellect, her status. For nearly forty years I nursed resentment and frustration at what I perceived as her limitations and her lack of ambition. It wasn't about finding what she wanted, I realized. She had what she really wanted. Somehow, what she really wanted was me. I loved her so much in that moment, almost as much as I hated myself.

"Mom," I whispered, "why did you give up on your acting dream?"

"Oh, honey," she said with an admonishing giggle, "that was just a schoolgirl fantasy. I think I always knew that.

Then when I had you, the choice was easy. I wasn't a very good actress, but I could be a good mom. That I could do. I didn't give up on my dream. I just chose a different one."

"The moves? The jobs?"

She shrugged, the gesture reminding me of May with a painful, electric immediacy.

"It wasn't always easy for a girl who never finished school to find a job that could pay the bills and let me be home when you got off the bus," she said.

"I thought his checks took care of that."

"Your father made sure you had a roof over your head and that you had clothes and enough to eat," she replied. "He was never particularly concerned that the same was true for me."

My mother and I had never spoken like this before, so honestly and so candidly about things that mattered. Colleen Winters and underwear advice seemed a very long time ago. "And I always made sure you were in a school district that was good enough for you." She reached out a hand and touched my face, her pink skin smooth and cool against the heat of my cheek. "You were always so smart."

"Not always."

As it turned out, my mother was every bit the lover and the fighter my father had been. In her case, the fighting and the loving both had been for me. I'd been a self-absorbed idiot not to see it before. But it wasn't too late. *I might be a lousy lover*, I thought, *but I don't have to be a lousy son.* And maybe, just maybe, I had more loving and more fighting in me, too, if I could figure out how to find them. Maybe it wasn't too late for that, either.

"The cabin sold for good money," I said, taking a folded check out of my pocket and putting it on the table between us. "This is your share."

She started to reach out a hand but then pulled it back, shaking her head.

"No," she said. "No, I've gotten by without him for a long time. I don't want his money now."

"It's not his," I replied, pushing the green paper toward her. "It's mine. And I want you to have it. He would have wanted that too, I'm sure of it."

Slowly, almost reluctantly, my mother opened the check. Her eyes grew wide for just a moment; five hundred thousand dollars will do that to you. Then she folded it back up, though she didn't put it down.

"You always were a terrible liar," she told me.

An hour later, we hugged again in the doorway, not as long as before but just as fierce.

"I'll call more, mom. And I'll come to see you at Christmas, I promise." She held my face in her hands and as she smiled, it was her turn to cry, just a little.

"That would be nice, honey," she said, which of course meant *I love you.*

~~~

Returning to school was always a bit of a blessing and a curse both. Between the mind-numbing professional development seminars and departmental meetings introducing new staff and new policies, there was the usual chatter with colleagues about summertime travels and trials. This year, for the first time, I found myself grateful to be surrounded by so many familiar faces. Nancy Pailes, fifty and five feet and a voice like a bullhorn, trim and athletic like a middle-aged cheerleader, had taught freshman English in the classroom next door the entire time I'd been at Arcadia. When I saw her in the parking lot my first day back, she hugged me. She'd never hugged me before. I probably looked like I needed one. For years I'd been walking around cocooned in a kind of artificial confidence and misplaced superiority, behind sullen walls of diffidence and disinterest, walls designed to keep people out that had only ever kept me in. I thought about that night on the dock with May, when I told her I didn't really have any friends. *Maybe I should do something about that,* I thought.

More surprising than Nancy's welcome was what greeted me as I walked up the paved footpath to Casper Hall. Chrys was gone. The corner of the courtyard where the old tree had once stood in stoic patience, shading generations of lucky lovers and luckless writers, was now vacant. Not even the stump remained. The entire corner had been landscaped with new sod, and generic young azalea bushes lined the stone foundation of Casper.

"What the hell, Chrys," I sighed. *No more dryads for us.* Not even Odette Kiefer. Her mother had been called back to Luxembourg, or wherever, and taken her family with her. I'd have to find a new second baseman.

I trudged up the creaking wooden stairs and down the corridor to the same classroom I'd been assigned when I first came to Arcadia. It was the back-to-school job I enjoyed most, opening the boxes I packed up a few months earlier, unearthing décor accumulated over my decade of teaching on the second floor of Casper Hall. It wasn't long before my bust of Shakespeare was back in his usual all-seeing pulpit atop my tallest bookcase, and a fraying "Know Your Brontës" poster was hanging by the door. I was liberating my Hawthorne and Poe bookends from their newspaper wrappings when Phyllis Collingwood came to see me. I had known the Head of Arcadia was abroad in the corridors of Casper; I could hear her thick heels tapping out their baritone rhythm against the well-worn pine-board floors, so it was no surprise when she materialized in the doorway, as tall and angular and dour as ever. She always made it a point to see everyone during the few days we spent getting ready for the students to return, and it must have been my turn.

"Doctor Kendall," she said in that gravelly voice.

"Doctor Collingwood." I left my boxes and shifted a pile of books out of the way so I could sit on a corner of my desk.

"Batteries recharged?"

It was her stock question, one I heard every year I worked there. I suspected we all heard it. I always found it oddly trite and informal for her, but today for the first time I detected a slight sardonic note, and realized it was a sort of joke we were in on together.

"Not in the slightest," I replied. I glanced around at the half-organized classroom. Sun was streaming in through the windows in their old wooden frames caked with another coat of white paint. It was a hot day, but it wouldn't be long before the ancient radiators cranked up their skin-cracking heat. Casper wasn't as old as Tappan Hall but it was old enough, a stately aging broad of a red-brick building, sagging in her dotage but still handsome, still doughty, still formidable.

I love it here. I had thought about not coming back. I had thought about seeing how far the money from the sale of my father's cabin would carry me, briefly nurturing fantasies about traveling the world and seeing what other stories I might yet find inside me. But when I tried to picture my future without Arcadia, something always felt wrong. I knew now, sitting there, that it was because this was my home. This musty, cramped room on the second floor, with its rows of overflowing bookcases and low plaster ceiling, with its impending crowds of variously-motivated students, this was my scrotum. Any books I had to write, I would write here. And then I thought of Anh Meyer and I smiled. *My book's not the only one that needs writing.*

"This is where my batteries charge," I said.

"Good to hear it. We are glad to have you back, Doctor Kendall."

"Thanks," I said.

"You noticed our friend Chrysopeleia?"

"Of course," I replied. "What happened? I mean, why was it cut down."

"Rot," she said simply, leaning slightly against the door-jam. "During some routine pruning this spring our grounds crew found some structural weaknesses. As it turned out, the entire interior of the poor old thing was dead and rotten." She spread one long-fingered hand in a gesture of futility. "Best to take it down before it failed and damaged the building or walkways. Some things can't be saved, I'm afraid."

I nodded silently. If I tried to say anything, I knew tears would come, and I had no desire to cry in front of Phyllis Collingwood. After a moment the moist brick in my throat ebbed, and I managed to open my mouth.

"Nothing gold can stay," I murmured.

"Leave it to a Dartmouth man to quote Frost," she said, gently. "I know the old tree meant a lot to the family here, so we saved some of the healthy wood, and Señora Muñoz made a few of these. I thought you might like one." She reached into one of the deep pockets of her long gray knitted vest – Dr. Collingwood always had a vest or jacket, no matter the temperature – and produced a leaf. It was light in my hand when she gave it to me, and at first I thought it was a leaf from Chrys, lacquered and preserved. But it was firmer, less fragile. It was wood, painstakingly carved and sculpted into the shape of a living leaf, curved and veined and alive, with a rich emerald finish. It was beautiful.

"I knew Rosalia was a sculptor," I said. "I didn't know she was this talented."

"Many hidden talents among our faculty," Dr. Collingwood replied. "Doctor Kendall, one of these days you'll have to let me have a look at your novel."

"I'm not..." I began, the deflection instinctive and automatic, then laughed as Dr. Collingwood dropped her chin slightly and peered over her huge glasses at me with a look requesting that I not treat her like an idiot. "Yes, ma'am. Of course."

Dr. Collingwood started to leave, then turned back.

"Señora Muñoz only made eight of those leaves," she said. "You are part of this family, Doctor Kendall. Whether you like it or not." And then she was gone, the cadence of her heels echoing down the hall.

I gingerly placed the oak leaf on my desk. The sun from the window, sun that used to be all too often blocked by oak branches, shafted in and ignited a million pinpricks of muted reflection on the painted surface of the carving. A cloud passed overhead and the effect faded, the green becoming just green again.

Then leaf subsides to leaf. So Eden sank to grief...

I went back to my unpacking, my decorating, my nesting. When it came time to re-shelve the books, I was like a kid on Christmas morning. I liked that the students would come to my classroom and tell me about what they were reading and ask about books they might like. And so I kept democratic bookshelves – democratic but orderly, with none of Ruby Pierce's indiscriminate chaos. Homer and Virgil alongside Tolkien and Lewis, Chaucer, Voltaire, Austen. Cervantes, and Shelley (God, I loved teaching *The Modern Prometheus*) alongside Rowling. Across the pond, Dickinson, Melville, Twain, Faulkner, and Hemingway shared space with Riordan and Asimov and Blume. And Moss. As I slid a paperback copy of *The Meat Grinder* onto the shelf, I'll admit it got a little dusty in there. Yeah, for the first time, I'd decided to teach my father's work to my Advanced Placement seniors. *Welcome aboard, Dad. Time for you to meet my kids.*

~~~

On our second day back, I went to see Juliet in the newer building across campus where the science faculty plied their trade. Prehistoric Casper Hall was good enough for the humanities, in fact, there were generous alumni donors who made it clear they preferred the shopworn architecture of the building where classical knowledge was bestowed upon the next generation of acolytes. A museum is sufficient, even appropriate for the past. But physics and chemistry, the technology of tomorrow? That demands state of the art facilities, labs, computers, resources. And so about three years ago, with the enthusiastic investment of those same alumni, Arcadia erected McIlhenny Hall. It had enough red-brick on its skin to suggest a family resemblance to the rest of campus, but enough shiny steel protrusions and expanses of gleaming glass to evoke the modernity required for its pedagogic ambitions. It was a beautiful building, no question, at least in part because it was new. My father hated new buildings. "They don't smell like anything," he wrote, and "you can't trust a building with skylights or a revolving door."

I walked through the revolving door into the grand atrium, an indoor garden easily twice the size of the courtyard outside Casper, bathed in yellow sun-love through massive skylights forty feet above. There were trees inside (though no white oaks), and flowers and shrubs and brick pathways and severe-looking steel benches where students and faculty could come together to contemplate the eternal questions of what E equals and how many digits of pi you have to memorize to be taken seriously. On one brick outcropping was a large oil painting, in the style of Colonel Tappan up the hill, of a pudgy looking man with a neckbeard and receding hairline and a preposterously long silken bowtie. *Edmund McIlhenny*, read the bronze plate alongside, *Inventor, Gardener, Benefactor*. I always chuckled when I saw that. You know why the building is named after him? Because his great-grandchildren ponied up the dough for the naming rights. McIlhenny died in 1890, leaving behind the fortune he made as the first mass-producer and mass-marketer of Tabasco sauce. He didn't invent the stuff, it was a gift from a friend, a friend who probably swiped it from the Creole slaves on his New Orleans plantation. And he made it in Louisiana, not Maryland. Oh, he was also a civilian employee of the Confederate Army during the Civil War. I bet The Colonel would have had no use for Edmund McIlhenny. But his family money was as green as its peppers, and Arcadia was happy to cash the checks. This was Maryland, not Massachusetts or Georgia. Maryland was the northernmost province of the South and the southernmost province of the North. It didn't have the luxury of picking sides with history.

A broad concrete-and-brick staircase swept lazily up to the second floor where the Biology wing sprawled, a line of glass-fronted classrooms along a grand mezzanine overlooking the gardens. I paused briefly, both to take in the view and to delay finding Juliet. From this vantage point, even a scientific illiterate like me could see that the walkways below wound in the vague shape of a double helix. I tried to imagine an atrium at Casper Hall with a walkway shaped liked a diagrammed sentence or Mary Shelley's head. *We're lucky it's not shaped like a bottle of Tabasco.* It wasn't my first sortie into McIlhenny; I'd been here for the wine-and-cheese dedication and several times since to find Juliet during our brief...our brief what? Relationship? Affair? It hardly mattered. I was exhausted with labels and categories and thinking. I'd been thinking for forty years without a whole hell of a lot to show for it.

"Oscar?"

I turned to see Juliet coming out of her classroom. She must have seen me through the glass. I was probably lucky she didn't push me over the railing.

"Hi," I said. She was as pretty as ever. Prettier. Her long, thick tawny hair was up in that sloppy ponytail, accenting the curve of her neck. High rosy cheekbones, pert nose, full lips, lively brown eyes regarding me warily but not without concern. She was dressed casually, in sneakers and jogging pants and a yellow tee-shirt with a half-peeled banana on the front. She was younger than I remembered.

"Hi?" Hers was a question, no doubt, and one that certainly deserved an answer. I began with an apology.

"I'm sorry." I leaned back against the brushed-steel railing, my hands hanging by my sides. "Juliet, I wasn't fair to you."

She stood, arms crossed over her chest, and waited. *The falcon.* It wasn't going to be that easy.

"Juliet, I..." I hesitated. I wasn't here to reconcile or to rekindle our little romance. I didn't know what I wanted, but I knew it wasn't that. It wouldn't be that for a long time, with Juliet or with anyone. Maybe never. And then I knew.

"I could use a friend," I said.

CHAPTER THIRTEEN

I never did go back to Dr. Midge's office. I had no interest in learning the compound German word for "after your famous father dies a woman you think you love drowns herself". The therapy I needed came on the granite bench in front of Casper Hall, my old perch greeting me with the grudging forgiveness of a neglected lover. My ass and my blue pen and I had come home, and on that familiar granite seat we underwent a furious nine-week paroxysm of inspiration. I missed the shade from my old oak friend, but once Halloween rolled around I was grateful for the sun that never used to reach the bench. I wrote, and I taught, and I wrote. I was writing other people's stories but these were my words, my voice alongside theirs. Was it my best work? What does that even mean, *best*? What standards or metrics apply to the written word that allow us to make universal declarations that one work is inherently and absolutely superior to another? Look, I get it. There's shitty writing. I know, I have notebooks full of trite phrases and clumsy dialogue and tepid plots. I teach writing to high school kids, for Chrissakes. Somewhere a line exists between good writing and bad writing. There's Jane Austen and there's Stephenie Meyer. But once you get into the legit stuff, a lot of the critique and rankings are purely subjective. A few years back the Baltimore Ravens were in the Super Bowl. A lot of my colleagues at Arcadia were jazzed up about it, and our athletic director had a big party at his house for the game. I was sitting on a couch, eating Doritos and nursing an obligatory Corona when a Ravens receiver dropped an important pass. "He sucks," someone said. *Sucks?* This was a guy who caught hundreds of balls in college, was drafted in the first round, and had scored something like thirty or forty touchdowns in the NFL. *Sucks?* You go do it then, asshole. I think about that whenever I read book critics or movie reviews. At the end of the day, I ask my students, did it speak to you?

Did it do so with some artistry? When I set my pen down in the middle of November, I didn't know if what I had written over the previous months was anything special. But it was mine. I had embraced my monster.

Lots of people like to cook but nobody does dishes as a hobby, so I won't bore you with the weeks of editing and revision that followed the writing. By Christmas break, I flew to Manhattan with two finished manuscripts in my leather shoulder bag. My father's literary agent worked at the venerable firm of Wheeler & St. Jean, Ltd., with offices on East 40th Street between Madison and Park, across from the Mexican Consulate. I walked the three blocks from Grand Central, buffeted by the kind of winter winds that can careen through the manmade canyons of New York City in December. I felt far from the lake, from the summer, from May, as a light snow began to fall. It was an older building, fifteen stories of wood and concrete and glass, the higher floors retreating from the street like stairs. A Portuguese market and a 24-hour locksmith flanked the heavy glass doors of #228. It was almost as cold inside as out, the walls and floor of the lobby all polished white marble with black veins and shiny metallic fixtures. I took the elevator to the tenth floor, where Wheeler & St. Jean, Ltd. had been flacking writers since the forties.

To my relief it was warmer there, handsome wood paneling and thick burgundy carpets that looked as though they hadn't been changed in decades. A young black woman with stylishly oversized glasses and a lovely apocalypse of jheri curls behind a heavy wood desk greeted me with professional geniality and asked how she could help me.

"I'm Oscar Kendall," I said. "Here to see Ginger Greene."

"I'm Joy," she replied with a broad smile, and I believed her. I'd never seen a smile with quite so many teeth. She checked something on her monitor, presumably a schedule. What she saw there must have confirmed my legitimacy because she looked up with another gleaming smile. They could have bottled Joy's smile and powered Manhattan for months. "Ms. Greene will be with you in a moment. Can I get you anything? Water, coffee?"

"No, thanks." I knew for a mortal certainty that I would spill coffee on my pants. I was nervous enough without courting that kind of high-percentage disaster.

"I'm sorry for asking," she asked in a tone that suggested Joy was seldom sorry for anything she said or did, "but Isaiah Moss was your father?"

"Yes." I smiled, with less wattage than Joy emitted. "And that's fine. I don't mind." I found, saying it, that it was true.

"What was he like?" Joy was pretty, but even had she been the spitting image of the Thing from the Black Lagoon, her effervescence would have made her magnetic. I liked her.

"Have you read his books?" I asked.

"Some of them."

"Then you know as well as I do. You and I have now spent as much time together as he and I did." I shrugged. I then asked her a question I had never asked anyone before. "Do you have a favorite?"

"*Ashes of Remorse*," she replied immediately. "My American Lit professor assigned it sophomore year at Ithaca. I remember thinking the last thing I wanted to read was another old white guy, you know? But that last line...*the mist of the soul is a hollow ache*...I've never forgotten it. *The mist of the soul*. A pain nothing can touch, blocking the sun, a bottomless hole."

I wondered what kind of pain a radiant creature like Joy could be hiding. I thought of May, of the agony in her heart, the mist shrouding her soul. *We never really know what private anguish resides in the people we meet*, I thought.

"That's a good one," I replied, and Joy smiled again. I wondered if her face ached when the day was over. I hadn't read *Ashes* for a long time, since graduate school. It was, improbably, a love story, a tale of romance between a Jewish woman and a Catholic man in Boston in the 1940s. The camp at Dachau claims her parents, D-Day his brothers. Instead of bringing them closer together, their tragedies drive them apart, into lives of solitary regret.

The world is wind, the passage reads in full, near the end of the book. *It comes on warm wings in summer, love and hope aborning, possibility and permission to believe. Cold too comes, in season, punitive and ruthless, unconcerned about what and who it cuts. In season, God willing. Sometimes the wheel is broken, and it will not turn. The season sticks. Pain lingers, shiftless, languid, overlong. Winter winds refuse to yield to the zephyrs of spring, and we die inside. Cold rain falls, without surcease, without succor. It falls, it falls, it drenches and freezes and rises again into a formless mist that arrests the marrow. It condenses into a white fog that enters us and suffuses us, replacing our heat with an everlasting chill. The mist of the soul is a hollow ache, a shadowed dell where snow never melts and summer never comes. It can be escaped. But it also cannot. Wind is unsolid, permeable, a prison only as we permit.*

I shuddered, the chill of the Manhattan winter still on me. *Korea?* I wondered, *or Chicago?* Where had my father become so intimate with winter? Or was the cold he wrote of distinct from the environment, a kind of spiritual winter that could and did descend regardless of latitudinal clime? I knew so little about the man himself, about the demons that drove him. I hadn't ever really thought much about *Ashes of Remorse,* or about the sequence that spoke to Joy the happy receptionist's inner turmoil. As a young man, it had seemed to me a standard lament of injury the world does us over time, of the depressive effect sustained pain can have on even the sunniest disposition, lodging us in a winter from which we can never free ourselves. Conjuring those lines now, I saw mostly the tincture of hope Isaiah Moss tucked into the corners of his prose. However dark, however deep, there is a way out if only we can find it. I smiled back at Joy.

"A prison only as we permit," I said, as if saying it would make me believe it.

A woman appeared in the hallway then, tall and thin, her hair probably once red but now steel-gray. She was fashionably dressed, a ruffled lavender blouse under a cream and green houndstooth wool vest and matching pencil skirt. Her heels were like javelins.

"Mr. Kendall," she said by way of greeting, reaching out with a perfectly manicured hand. "Good to see you again." We'd met just the once, in the spring, at the reading of my father's will. I felt fairly certain she'd needed an assistant, maybe the perfectly-named Joy, to brief her on who I was when I scheduled the appointment. Ginger Greene had no accent, no borough pugnacity or southern wallow or New England nose, just a vanilla voice designed to elicit nothing other than vague comfort. Ginger Greene was of indeterminate age, and indeterminate affect, a fleshly android programmed to sweet talk authors and hardball publishers, to sell books, to sell, to sell.

"Mrs. Greene," I answered, taking her hand. It was dry and warm and barely there, like shaking hands with a childhood summer's day.

"Ms." Ginger Greene smiled, which would probably have charmed me if she were twenty years younger or if I could still be charmed. As it was, I nodded by way of acknowledgement.

"My apologies. Ms. Greene. And it's Dr. Kendall, if you don't mind."

I hadn't planned on that, but her casually assumed superiority irked me, and setting her on those preposterous stilt-heels for the briefest of moments helped me quiet my clattering nerves.

"Of course. Dr. Kendall. Please, follow me."

I did as I was bidden, trailing her down the long ecru hallway, lined with the portraits of authors and book covers. My father was there, the Young Elvis, flanked by the first-edition cover art from *Club Lucky*. Generally considered this finest of the Moss novels (though there were devotees of *Holding Your Breath* and even *The Meat Grinder*), often judged as one of the ten greatest works of American literature, *Club Lucky* was an unflinching chronicle of the last days of the Chicago gangs, the death cries of the meat-packing industry, and the erosion of an American city. It was told through the eyes of Luisa Pastuszak, a young Polish good girl who became a mob accountant, a bootlegger, a racketeer, and eventually an FBI informant.

I've never read it, but I had seen the Blythe Danner movie. It was a nominee for Best Picture and Best Adapted Screenplay in 1975 (it didn't win either), and I thought it was fine, if a bit slow. Most movies serious enough to call themselves cinema are glacial to me. But then, I'm part of the easily-bored *Star Wars* generation. You've got to throw in some gratuitous explosions or nudity to hold our attention. At least Gwyneth Paltrow's mom took her shirt off a couple of times in *Club Lucky* or I might have nodded off. My father said he hated it (other than, presumably, Blythe's boobs), but he always said he hated the film adaptations of his novels. He never failed to cash the rights checks, though, and once he grumbled to me in a letter about the *Club Lucky* movie coming up against *Chinatown* and the second *Godfather* movie at the Oscars that year. "Organized crime had never been more organized," he wrote. It was the closest one of his books would come to a golden statuette. The old man would have to content himself in eternity with a Pulitzer and two National Book Awards. My favorite movie made from one of his books was Hollywood's 1991 treatment of *The Meat Grinder*, which despite the talents of Anthony Hopkins and Michael Douglas was labeled a flop. I saw it in the theater, and I liked it because I was fourteen and there was a body count.

Ginger Greene's office was exactly what I had expected. Extravagant, opulent, posh – name your adjective applicable to conspicuous consumptive luxury. One wall was entirely windows, admitting a panoramic view of East 40th Street and the city beyond, the kind of view executives regardless of industry liked as a suggestive inference of power. There was a big desk devoid of paper, just a sleek, blue-tinted Mac of the latest iteration perched in solitary snobbery. *How would people know how hip you were if you didn't have some Jobsian idol on your desk?* I wondered. A few shelves held up engraved clear acrylic awards that must have meant something. There was a well-stocked wet bar along one stretch of mahogany cabinets, and the sitting area had couches upholstered in even deeper shades of brown. *Rich Corinthian leather*, I thought in Ricardo Montalban's voice. Except there's no such thing as Corinthian leather, Athenian leather, Spartan leather, Ithacan leather. It's just marketing make-believe Chrysler came up with and asked Montalban to say in their 1970's commercials for the LeBaron and Cordoba. *That shit is made in New Jersey.* Wheeler & St. Jean, Ltd. was the phoniest place I'd been outside of the District of Columbia, and I was going there next.

"Please, sit."

I sat. The couch was unbelievably comfortable. *Those guys in New Jersey know their business.* Where the granite of Casper Hall's bench and the Great Testicle were unyielding, the sofa cushions gave way like the pillows of a hotel bed, like the lips of a willing woman. It felt fondling and familiar and not a little wrong. Ginger perched erect and prim in a straight-backed chair of polished wood to my left, nyloned legs crossed with practiced ease. She turned slightly at the waist so her knees pointed away from me while her narrow shoulders addressed me squarely. Everything about Ginger Greene was thin, from her slender torso to her penciled eyebrows to the fleshless fingers she folded on her thin lap to the wire frames on her stylish glasses. I wondered if she needed them or if they were affectation.

"Can I get you anything? Did the girl offer you coffee, or water?"

"Yes, Joy was very welcoming. But I'm fine, thanks." I couldn't tell if *the girl* was a standard-issue dismissal of a subordinate by a senior executive or Ginger's way of establishing a similarly elevated role relative to me. For some reason I had the feeling that it hadn't been unknown for Isaiah Moss to refer to me between them as *the boy* in a similar way. I was almost certain Ginger Greene's legs hadn't always been crossed like that for my father, back when her gray hair had still been red.

"Good." She adjusted her glasses slightly. *Yup,* I thought, *affectation.* Just like the kids at Arcadia with their empty hipster frames. *She's as fake as the leather on the couch. Rich Corinthian Ginger.* "Then how can I help you, Dr. Kendall?"

I caught myself about to say she could call me Oscar. I realized I was okay with Dr. Kendall. I'd been Mr. Kendall to my students for years now, and I was forty-three years old. The only way to cease being *the boy* is to cease being the boy. I decided I'd give Phyllis Collingwood an early Christmas present and start calling myself Dr. Kendall in the classroom. Doctor Coach Kendall was just as good as Mister Coach Kendall. *Better, even.*

"It's about my father's will."

"I thought it was fairly straightforward," Ginger said, adjusting her glasses again.

"Oh, it was," I replied. "The will refers rights and royalties to all previously published works by Isaiah Moss to the trust. The cabin and its contents were left to me."

"Yes."

"Well, this was in the cabin." I reached into my bag and withdrew the manuscript I had found my first night at the lake. I laid *The Last Sane Man,* by Isaiah Moss, on the glossy table.

Ginger stared at the stack of unbound bond paper, now slightly dog-eared. Her face was expressionless as she reached out a slender hand toward it then stopped, took off her glasses, and rubbed her eyes with a forefinger and thumb. Her nails were long and immaculate and lavender, like her blouse. *And probably fake like her glasses.*

"You found this in the cabin?" she asked, laying the glasses on the table. The veneer of icy dispassion dissolved, replaced by a look of primal and predatory hunger with just a hint of skepticism.

"I did."

"And you've read it." She was leaning forward now, not looking at me but at the manuscript. It lay there on the table like some ancient relic Indiana Jones had unearthed from a vine-choked jungle temple, an arcane artifact of latent unknown power.

"Every word."

"And..."

"And it's genuine, Ms. Greene. It's more than genuine. It's genius."

In one smooth, unhurried motion Ginger picked it up. With the ease born of inspecting thousands of manuscripts over her career, she placed the first sheet face down on the table and then the second. She swiftly absorbed the opening paragraphs, but before a couple of minutes had gone by she replaced the top pages and looked out the sprawling windows with an inscrutable look on her face. I knew what she was feeling. I had felt the same way months before in the cabin, when I knew what I was reading. Awe. Reverence.

And so I waited.

"He left something for you," she said.

While her voice retained its nurtured neutrality, the ghost of confusion danced across her narrow face like the shadow of a high cloud over a sun-drenched meadow. Still clutching the embryonic book like the child I was pretty sure she'd never had, Ginger stood and walked briskly to her desk. She reached into a drawer and withdrew a small envelope, the size of a postcard. She handed it to me. On the envelope, in a hasty script, was handwritten "The Boy."

"His instructions were that you should only have this if you brought me something of his." I could tell she was as bewildered as I was. For an instant I wondered if she had any idea if this was what the old man had intended, or if she had expected a more personal memento of some kind. I also realized with an odd twinge that it was the first time I had ever seen his handwriting. My curiosity taking hold, I broke the glue on the envelope and took out the single sheet of crisp white paper it held. All but one word was typewritten.

Oscar,

This is my last letter to you. My last words to anyone. I write it more for me than for you, which if nothing else should win me points for consistency. Everything I ever did was for me.

I will admit that I have been a shitty father. In all fairness to me, I never set out to be a father at all, so shitty is better than nonexistent. At least I tried a little, which is more than they can say for stray cats. I write this not by way of apologia. I'm not sorry. I lived my life as I chose, which is its own kind of courage.

I didn't leave you the royalties to my work because you didn't earn them. Some days I wake up and believe that no one has ever put words to paper as brilliantly as I have, and that I have been a modern Homer, a Shakespeare, a Voltaire. And on other days, I know it's a bunch of bullshit. I was a man in the end, with flaws and vices and appetites and a talent for storytelling. As a boy, I loved. As a man, I knew better. I never loved your mother, I never loved you, I never loved myself. I never loved the world. What is love, but avarice and conceit? I don't love. But I remember.

I was nineteen in Korea. I'd never known a woman, but a lot of the guys I served with had. They loved, oh, how they loved. At night around the fires of our camps they would show me the little photographs they carried, blurry black-and-white Beryls and Helens and Ruths. They would tell me how they couldn't wait to get back home to their love. Their love didn't save them when the gunfire rained down or when winter came, just like love didn't do shit for my father at Monte Cassino. I didn't love. Did that save me? Probably not. Other guys didn't have wives or sweethearts and the bullets pierced them and the frostbite ate their feet all the same. Love didn't save or damn, Life isn't love. Life is luck.

I remembered them, and I made their stories mine, and I gave the lucre from my earthly efforts to the men who sleep in the ground outside Inchon, who drowned in the Yalu, who bled and burst and wept on the Peninsula in the cold. I remember their faces, and their stories, and the photographs they carried. I've been trying to forget them for seventy years, writing as purgative, but they remember me, too. And soon I will have to answer to them. Too soon.

And I remember you, too, and I answer to you before I go. I left you the cabin because it is a place where miracles happen. Secular miracles, godless miracles, miracles of our own begetting. I have never wished you love, or success, or riches. I wish you only this: that if there is a miracle in you, that you have the courage to find it. And that maybe you find just a little luck, too, before we meet again.

And he had signed it, not with the standard typed I. Moss with which he had concluded each of his previous letters to me, but with the scrawled, unfamiliar word "Dad".

Something in my gut lurched, and I set the letter down. I was vaguely aware of Ginger Greene in the room, sitting at her desk, thumbing through the last great novel of Isaiah Moss, caressing each page as if it were a gold doubloon, which I suppose it was. I didn't really care. It wasn't mine. I mean, legally it was mine, but it wasn't *mine*. No more than I was his.

"I assume you want the book." I was surprised at how calm I sounded. At how calm I felt.

"Is it yours to give?" Ginger asked. The skepticism was gone from her gaze, leaving just the predation. I spread my hands.

"Yes." Mine to yield up, not mine to claim. "It was among the contents of the cabin. It's not a published work of Isaiah Moss. I'm not an expert in property or inheritance law, but that seems pretty straightforward to me."

Ginger scowled. Her face was so narrow that the expression was almost comical. I took her silence to mean that particular point was settled.

"I'd be a fool to just give away something that valuable," I continued. "I mean, what's a sure-fire #1 bestseller worth these days, anyway? The last work of a literary titan? A million dollars? Five? Ten? Fifty?"

"Not fifty," she replied, and I found myself grinning.

"Don't worry, Ms. Greene. I'm not here looking for money. Not for me, anyway. That manuscript belongs to the Moss estate, and the proceeds will go to the Korean War Memorial as my father intended."

"Is that what he says in that letter?"

"It is if you speak Isaiah Moss," I said, picking the note back up, folding it neatly in half and slipping it into my pocket. "Oh, and he wanted a dedication," I lied. "*For Ruby Pierce, the Last Sane Woman.*"

"Anything else you want, Dr. Kendall?"

I reached into my satchel again and produced the other manuscript I had brought with me. My manuscript.

"A little luck," I said, placing *Wages of Empire* on the table.

~~~

After New York, I headed to Washington. I had two stops left to make, and both were in the nation's capital, a convenient hour from my apartment in Maryland. It was one of those brisk days you get on the Mall in wintertime, with wind whistling from the Potomac past Lincoln and across the drained Reflecting Pool on its keening path to the Capitol. Not many tourists braved the chill weather, which was fine by me. I wasn't a huge fan of the sweaty crowds on a hot Washington Saturday, all jostling from their Metro stairwell to whatever memorial or museum was on their list for the afternoon in their crocs and tank tops. I folded up the collar of my overcoat, jammed my hands in my pockets, and trudged through the slush. I preferred the slush to the crowds.

In the morning, I went to the Smithsonian's American History Museum to meet with the curator responsible for acquisitions related to cultural holdings. She was all too happy to accept the typewriter Isaiah Moss used to write his legendary novels, though she expressed mild regret that a couple of the keys were missing. She wasn't interested in the cufflinks, so I kept them. If you ever want to see the Remington, they've got it there. I guess it's become something of a favorite in the exhibit on American authors, between one of Hemingway's hats and a first-edition Melville. They've even got a LEGO version you can buy in the gift shop. I can't imagine Isaiah Moss would have cared much for that. After all, words were all the toys he ever needed.

After lunch, I went to my last stop, a bit further down the Mall.

Everyone talks about the Vietnam Veterans Memorial, and with good cause. The Wall is a deeply humbling experience. The simplicity of the engraved names and overwhelming bulk of their number, the way the shining stone nestles sheepishly, almost forgotten, into the earth has none of the arrogant grandeur of Lincoln on his throne or Washington's sky-piercing obelisk. The Wall is not a place of braggadocio, not a strutting emblem of American exceptionalism. It exudes a certain shamefacedness alongside these more traditional symbols, a reluctance to draw attention to itself, a self-awareness that the nation that erected it remains conflicted about what it represents. There is no pomp or pride, only an all-pervasive sense of grief and waste. Black Indian granite, polished to a high sheen, it reflects the weather, the season, and the visitor with mirrorlike clarity. The ache of bereaved widows, the solemnity of foreign tourists, the hesitant curiosity of children; the polished surface of the Memorial includes what comes to it.

Casual visitors and earnest seekers alike are often confused as the names are listed not alphabetically but chronologically, beginning in the center with 1959 and running east for 70 panels toward the Capitol before carrying on at the far western end and finishing in the middle with 1975. The last and first lost are eternal neighbors there, an alpha and omega of futility. Most in search of an individual name will do their research ahead of time online or else use the printed directory nearby. It is a thick book. I found what I was looking for there: panel 3E, not far to the right of the modest center apex of the Wall. About two thirds of the way down, Langdon F. Pierce was engraved. A diamond was next to his name, indicating he was killed in action and his body was recovered. A plus sign meant they were still missing, while a circle meant they had been presumed missing but came home alive. I read in the directory that there were still 1,500 plus signs. And no circles.

I didn't know what the F. stood for.

Not far away on the National Mall is the memorial to the other war America would most often prefer to forget. But while the American tragedy in Vietnam spawned a generation of poets to lament and to immortalize, the Korean War had the ill luck to be born too soon for hippie protest anthems or beatnik verse prosecution. The Vietnam generation had George Harrison and Joan Baez and Allen Ginsberg. The men who fought in Korea had their older brothers who had stormed Normandy and liberated Dachau and stared down Hirohito. The men who fought in Korea had MacArthur vs Truman, they had confusion and uncertainty. Over 58,000 Americans died in Vietnam over nearly 20 years. In Korea, over 36,000 died in less than four. While we work harder each year to remember our Vietnam vets, each year we forget our Korean vets a little more.

The Korean War Memorial isn't abstract or mind-numbing the way the Wall is. It's not a rebuke to a nation, an obsidian scar ripped ragged across a green sward. It's gentler, unironic, and somehow even sadder. It's just men. Men trudging through snows of bronze and rivers of hedge, lit from below in simple remembrance, toward some goal they will never attain. It's a Sisyphean exercise in unresolved, elegiac striving. I sat in the cold on one of the marble benches put there for the purpose. It was overcast, with an unseen sun yawning to retirement behind the Potomac basin to my left, and the gathering dark suited the place. These were men accustomed to the dark. Their timeworn and timeless faces stared back at me with a patient lack of reproach, resignedly mute.

If there was a national memorial to the wars in Iraq and Afghanistan, I would have gone there too. But there aren't. *There will be someday.*

I reached into a pocket of my overcoat. Even through the leather of my glove, the small bottle of Jim Beam was hard and cold inside the crackling brown paper bag. I screwed off the top and took a sip. Just a small one, a last one. I knew I'd never drink Jim Beam again. Then I quietly emptied what remained in four slow pours onto that hallowed ground.

Clayton Moss losing his life near Monte Cassino, Langdon Pierce losing his at Ia Drang. Isaiah Moss losing his innocence at Inchon. May Pierce losing her legs and future at Jalalabad. *Ah, May.* God, it still ached when I thought of her. I dreaded the day when I woke without that ache. The ache was her still with me, if only a little.

Clayton, Langdon, Isaiah, May. Each graven eye in the statues before me told of those losses and more, and more, and more than more. I put the bag with the empty bottle back into my pocket. From my other pocket, I took out a little Ziploc bag. Inside was what was left of my father. I opened the bag and scattered the teaspoon or so of ashes into the ground where I'd spilled the whiskey.

"Don't worry Dad," I said. "I gave most of you to the lake, like you wanted. But I didn't think you'd mind if some of you rested here, too. Just a bit. Maybe the best bit. Maybe just your heart." That was the only moment when I thought I might crack, but I didn't. "Don't worry. I'm pretty sure I left your balls at the cabin." I stood, breathing out in long white trails of smoke. "Well, ball."

I tried to think of something else to say, but I'd already said it all. I nodded to the soldiers frozen in their perpetual march, then turned and walked away. They might not have loved me, but I loved them. My grandfather, who never stopped loving his country. Langdon F. Pierce, who died before I was born. My father, who considered every day of his life a debt to the men he served with, writing with a feverish need to pay it back. May, too late for both of us. *Ah, May.* I would live, and love, as best I could. And I would remember.

A light breeze began to blow, and a surprisingly gentle gust blew a leaf against my chest where it clung like an importunate kitten. It was an oak leaf from the previous fall, brown and dry and yet flawlessly shaped. Plato would have admired its essential Leafness. It crumbled in my hand no matter how gently I held it, cracking and fragmenting until it was gone in the wind like my breath.

Moss

Nature's first green is gold,
Her hardest hue to hold.
Her early leaf's a flower;
But only so an hour.
Then leaf subsides to leaf.
So Eden sank to grief,
So dawn goes down to day.
Nothing gold can stay.

I fingered my cufflinks. First the left, then the right.
Round, white, time-worn. Bold black letters in the middle.

About the Author

Joe Pace is a New Hampshire native and recovering political scientist. His wife Sarah is an Army veteran and doctor. Their sons are 12 and 14, their dogs somewhat younger. Joe has previously published two science fiction novels: *Minotaur* (2012) and *Lost Harvest* (2015), both through Reliquary Press.

Photo by Paul Royal, Art & Science Photography

CPSIA information can be obtained
at www.ICGtesting.com
Printed in the USA
BVHW061409271221
624935BV00011B/469